THE ALL SEASONS GARDENER

PENGUIN BOOKS

Mark Cullen is Canada's leading gardening expert, reaching over 2 million Canadians every week through his extensive media work. His education in horticulture began during his childhood in the family gardening business; he is now President of Weall & Cullen Garden Centres throughout Southern Ontario. He is the resident garden expert on CFRB 1010 Radio in Toronto and his weekly "Garden Show" is syndicated across the country on fourteen radio stations. As well as appearing weekly on "Canada AM" with co-host Dan Matheson, Mark hosts his own TV show, "Right in Your Own Backyard," on Home and Garden Television and is the gardening expert on "Canadian Living TV." He also writes a weekly gardening column for *The Sunday Sun* in Toronto.

Mark Cullen is the bestselling author of *A Greener Thumb* and co-author of *The Real Dirt*, both published by Penguin Books Canada.

Introduction

The nineties, we were told, would be the decade of innovation. More uses for the computer chip, for example, would be found than anyone had thought imaginable just a few years ago. Why, I can't take my car in to the corner garage for a routine oil change without getting hooked up to a sophisticated computer-driven diagnostic think tank.

So it is with gardening. Kind of. My collection of antique gardening books date themselves by their references to deadly chemicals that were long ago replaced by environmentally friendly products. (Can you imagine using nicotine arsenate or DDT today!) Fertilizers, plant names, even plants themselves have changed — they've been hybridized by plant breeders to the point that today's versions hardly resemble the original great-grandparent. Today's hybrid roses are a perfect example. If they were put side by side, you would have trouble recognizing that the original species is related in any way to the modern varieties. This is progress.

As plant breeders have progressed with the introduction of new and improved plants for the past three or four hundred years, so have growing *methods* improved. We very often don't use soils, but soilless mixes; we use electronic timers to water, power mowers (*mulching* mowers), tillers, blowers, chippers/shredders, weed whippers, hedge trimmers, and you get the picture.

What this book is all about is harnessing this innovation and this information, and putting them to work for you. This book organizes the labour-saving, season-extending, and effective growing techniques of the day so that you can benefit. Year-round.

This book celebrates the diversity of the four gardening seasons we are blessed with here in Canada. It harnesses the life-giving energy of the sun — in January!

Enjoy yourself!

Mark
Merchant of Beauty

How To Use This Book

The All Seasons Gardener contains lots of stories, but it's not a storybook.

It will serve a purpose for many as a handy reference guide by month, by season, and by garden activity, but it's not encyclopedic. It *is* a guide to gardening year-round. Indoors, outdoors, with kids, with new tools and innovative gardening solutions, and with some long-forgotten, but tried-and-true, garden activities.

When you have time, open it anywhere. Refer to the monthly checklist at the end of each chapter for useful reminders of what needs to be done.

You'll find specific how-to information, personal anecdotes, and stuff you can use. Always, stuff you can use.

My aim is to inspire you, inform you, and entertain.

When you're in a hurry, use the index.

Winter

THE EXPRESSION "IN SEASON" HAS TAKEN ON A NEW meaning. Many Canadians will remember years ago when fresh fruits and vegetables were available "in season," which meant the period of time during which locally grown produce was ripe. The growing season *was* the selling season, with the exception of some produce that kept well (like rutabagas and turnips). Menus tended to be governed according to the laws of nature.

Today, of course, we enjoy strawberries in winter, apples in spring, and peaches in fall. (Mind you, I feel that the midwinter tomatoes they strip-mine down in Texas leave a lot to be desired.) Thanks to recently improved cultivars, growing and storage techniques, and efficient transportation systems, we can eat just about any fruit or vegetable we choose (sometimes for a handsome price!) any time of year.

So it is with gardening. If you enjoy getting your fingers dirty, as I do, if you enjoy the lovely musty smell of damp soil *all year*, and if the colour and fragrance of spring make you feel like a carefree youth (again), you'll love this section. Here we show you how to bring many of the pleasures of spring home early and how to prepare your garden for a healthy, bountiful year.

Follow the advice given here and I don't guarantee you will avoid the typical midwinter Canadian cold or flu. I *do* guarantee, however, that the increased humidity in your home from young seedlings in sunny windows or under lights, and the variety of early-spring projects suggested here, will make your suffering much more bearable.

And, I hasten to add, the kids will love helping you out — getting them involved now is the secret to a year-round interest in gardening for them. Consider your time and effort as an investment in the future.

Chapter 1

January

Winter's Chill and Gardener's Plans

Rule of Thumb

Snow acts as insulation for most of the garden, but heavy wet snows are damaging to evergreen trees, whose branches often snap under the weight. Throughout the winter, gently brush snow off laden limbs.

This is the time of year when nongardeners offer sympathy to their gardening friends—after all, the harvest has been gathered, the garden has been tidied, and there's probably snow on the ground! Don't let those nongardeners fool you— there's lots to do, and you may even be able to delight friends with some treats from your winter garden. Besides, the gardening season isn't really *over* —the first seed catalogues are about to be delivered. Now is the time to start ordering!

With less to do *in* the garden, you can get caught up on garden-related activities, such as horticultural reading; cleaning, sharpening, repairing, and oiling your garden tools; or taking some gardening courses. This is also the time of year to look at your garden with a critical eye and to start dreaming about and planning for the coming season.

Planning Your Garden

Winter can be an unforgiving time of year for assessing your garden—but an important one. During the winter months you can see your garden's bare bones: the patterns made by paths, gates, decks, fences, flower beds, shrubs, and trees. As plants die back and leaves fall, the relationship between space, plantings, and objects in the garden will become clear. If something about the layout of your garden has been bothering you during the summer season but you haven't quite figured out what the problem is, this is likely the time of year you'll suddenly understand what it is. Take advantage of winter's clean slate by planning your garden in this season.

An additional benefit of planning at this time of year is that you will be more aware of adding winter colour and interest to your garden design than if you were to do it in the spring, when it's all too easy to forget the relative barrenness of the winter garden. Remember, too, that during the winter you will usually be viewing your garden only from the house. Your views will be restricted to those from your windows, so you want those views to be especially attractive in the winter. As you gaze out the window, reach for pencil and paper and start making notes.

Light and shade produce different effects in the summer and winter garden. Visualize plant material and decorative and practical structures as they might look at different seasons when you plan your garden. Don't forget that the sun's rays fall at differing angles with the changing seasons.

The New Garden

You've just moved into a new subdivision or you've bought a house with nothing but lawn surrounding it. You're like an artist sitting in front of a blank canvas. I can remember tracing the shape of flower beds in the snow with my foot when I was a young landscape designer. It was like designing a giant living canvas.

There are two ways of approaching this canvas, your new garden: as a plant collector or as a patient artist. The first approach is often dictated by the plants you want. As you thumb through books and magazines and remember the names of flowers you saw in friends' gardens, you make a list of all the things you want to grow. In the spring the newly purchased plants are tucked into their new beds, often with not much forethought. The fun of this type of nonplanning is its spontaneity, the collecting of new plants, the continual change. Over the years, you move things around as you see that colours clash, heights aren't right, or you just don't like that rose bush in that spot. There's nothing wrong with this approach — it's your garden, after all, and you probably have a lot of fun moving things around and experimenting.

Winter gives you the time to attend to necessary maintenance so you're ready for the busy gardening season coming up. (ABOVE) *putting a clean edge on a garden spade;* (BELOW) *sharpening secateurs for early spring pruning.*

If you want your garden to give you pleasure year-round, though, you should consider the second approach. It's longer term, but ultimately more satisfying. Don't make any major decisions for as much as a year. That's a long time for an eager gardener to wait, but the time spent planning will repay you.

As you ponder your "garden canvas" throughout the year, think of the ways you want to use your garden, and consider your priorities. An exercise that will help you focus is to complete the sentence that starts "I want to use my garden as ... " You might finish it with "a playground for the children," or "a place to grow vegetables," or "a bird sanctuary." Once you know what you want your garden to be, you can embark on fulfilling the dream. (If you truly want a garden to suit your children, let them have a hand in the design — it may release the child within you.)

Note how shadows fall differently with the seasons: the delicate lines of maple-tree branches in winter turn to solid shade in July. Get out a camera and take shots of the garden space at different times of the year, in different weather and light conditions. Look at other people's gardens and plantings and notice how plants such as evergreens and heathers that you are scarcely aware of in the summer months become focal points in the winter.

Keep copious notes and photographs for visual reference — your goal for this year of planning is to evaluate your garden site and learn its character and qualities.

Once you've assessed your garden throughout the changing seasons, you can begin to draw up plans. On grid paper and using a dark pencil, do a scale drawing of your property, showing the house and any other existing features (such as sheds, paths, trees, and other plantings). Make several photocopies of your scale drawing. This will give you extras for designing what I call a "phased garden" — each sketch represents the plantings and features you will add season by season or year by year.

On your grid sheet, you can start to add, subtract, and move around the elements that will be in the garden. You may go through several versions as you work out places for your flower beds, the vegetable garden, the pond, the herb garden, the compost pile.

A separate but related and important step is to decide on your plantings — what you're going to put in those beds, the plant materials you'll use for hedges, the vine to disguise an eyesore. Imagine what your plants will look like when they're fully grown. Sit down with books and magazines and talk to friends as you ponder colour combinations, heights of mature plants, your soil conditions, your climate, and the

amount of time you're willing to spend on upkeep. I'll be describing some plants throughout this book, but there are many other books devoted to specific topics and plants — perennials, annuals, vines, shrubs, trees, vegetables, even entire books on roses, irises, and lilies, among others.

Getting all those elements to work together in a pleasing design can be an enjoyable challenge. You need to balance the horticultural requirements of your plant material with design considerations of line, form, colour, texture, rhythm, perspective, and scale. Aim to have colour through as many weeks of the year as possible, but don't overlook the valuable part foliage plants such as grasses, ferns, and evergreens play. In gardening, the line between exuberance and restraint is a fine one. You want to achieve peace in a garden while maintaining a sense of joy and movement, all expressed through plants and their relationship to one another.

Once you've settled on your design, plantings, and colour combinations, get some onionskin or other see-through paper to place over your base design. Use a sheet for each season and colour in your plantings as if the flowers were in bloom. This will help you see where you need added interest.

It's easy to forget from one season to the next how lush growth can be, or how bare branches can open up a view. Keep a photographic record of your garden through the year from the same point of view to help you see where you can make improvements.

Winter interest in the garden can be as planned as an attractive spruce (ABOVE LEFT), or as serendipitous as a late rose that has dried on the stem (RIGHT).

Renovating Your Garden

In fact, most of us don't start with a "blank slate" when it comes to planning a garden. We've inherited someone else's garden and we want to make it our own. Renovating a garden that isn't quite right can be a difficult task, but one advantage is that you already know its good points and its bad points. If you've been working in this garden for several seasons, you'll know where the sun falls throughout the year, what the soil is like, where the exposed and sheltered parts of the garden are, what your zone and your own microclimate are (see more about zones and microclimates in Chapter 2) — and, perhaps most important, you know a bit about what plants do well in your garden and which struggle to survive.

As with planning a new garden, make a scale drawing of your property and ask yourself the same kinds of questions about how the garden will be used. Decide how extensive the renovation will be. Will you do the landscaping yourself or hire someone to do it? Will you spread the job over several years, either because of the labour or expense involved, or do it all at once? Review the advice in the previous section on designing the new garden, for many of the same principles apply.

Part of the planning process will involve deciding the best time of year to undertake the renovation. If you're like me, you'll want to rush outside on the first nice day and get going, but making some scheduling decisions now will help you focus on what's best for your garden and plants when you finally hunker down to work. Generally, the best times to renovate are spring and fall; however, you'll want to avoid digging when the ground is wet, because this can destroy the structure of the soil. Perennials can be divided and replanted in the spring, although you won't always get blooms the same year. If you're renovating the garden in fall, divide perennials about a month before a killing frost so the roots have a chance to become established before winter. The fall is also a good time to dig new beds, turning the sod over and piling compost on the bed until the spring, when you can just shake off the clods before adding them to the compost pile.

Planning Tips

Here are some things you should consider as you draw up your plan for establishing a new garden or renovating an existing one. First, some ideas to help extend the season.

- Try to make room for a little spring sun trap in your design. Look for a corner of the garden that catches the sun and warms up early in the year. A natural sun trap is a spot where the snow melts first and green shoots appear before anywhere else. I found our garden's sun trap by watching the cat — she found the ideal spot for a nap. You can help a sunny corner warm up even more quickly if you install a few rocks to absorb the heat and radiate it back to the soil and plants. Sun traps near walls and paving will also warm up fast because of this principle. In the fall, plant some early-flowering bulbs in the sun trap for an end-of-winter treat. It's a bonus if your sun trap is visible from a window of the house, so don't obscure the view from the house with tall plantings.
- See if you can work in space for even a small cold frame (see page 31) for hardening off (see Chapter 4) seedlings or for use with vegetables. If you expect to use the cold frame over the winter, keep it as close as possible to the house, ideally against a south-facing brick wall out of the northwest wind. The heat absorbed by the wall will radiate into the cold frame.
- Consider making some of your beds, especially vegetable beds, raised. (See more about this subject in Chapter 3.)

Now for some practical considerations

- **Shade:** What is the movement of the sun, not only during the day, but at different times of the year? Will some trees have to be pruned or completely sacrificed, a hedge cut back, a fence moved to let more light into the garden? Unfortunately, the question of what to do about shade-producing structures such as houses and garages — especially those belonging to neighbours — can't be answered as easily!
- **Winds:** Where are the prevailing winds from? Will you need to plant a windbreak such as a hedge? Where are the sheltered spots of the garden and how can you use them to extend your growing season?
- **Water:** Where do you keep your hose? Where are the water outlets? Are there water shortages in your area? Can you afford an automatic watering system?
- **Storage:** Where will you keep the lawn mower, rakes, shovels, clippers, watering cans, wheelbarrow, flowerpots, fertilizers? Is your collection of tools and garden aids likely to increase over the years?

Rule of Thumb

If you're adding structures such as a new deck, a wall, a pergola, or trellis, have them constructed in the spring or fall before you start to add or move plants.

A crocus can survive the snow — and so can the gardener! Find a protected sunny spot for planting and be rewarded with early blooms.

The wide variety of textures and shapes of paving material makes it easy to add interest to your garden.

When planning the garden, think beyond borders, shrubs, and trees. Decide on locations for accents that can change every year. This wheelbarrow can have a different combination of colours and shapes from year to year. Shown (RIGHT) are geraniums, begonias, coleus, asparagus fern, ivy, and dracena.

- **Garbage bins:** Where's the best place for the garbage bins? Outside the kitchen door? Near the front of the house?
- **Composting:** How sophisticated is your composting system? Do you use one compost bin or several? Is it a freestanding pile or contained? How close is it to your flower and vegetable beds? Will you be able to get to it in the winter?
- **Upkeep:** How much time are you willing to put into looking after the garden? How much grass do you really want to cut? How much pruning do you want to do? What low-maintenance plants are suitable for your zone?
- **The future:** How are your gardening interests and the uses of your garden likely to change through the years? How long do you expect to stay in this location? If not long, what low-cost, quick-growing plants can you include in your design?

And for the fun and beauty part

- **Recreation:** Do the children want a sandbox, swing set, climbing apparatus? Do you like to barbecue? How about a swimming pool? Are there places to sit and enjoy your garden?
- **Pets:** How will the family pet live with your garden? Is there a place that can be set aside for the dog?
- **Specialty gardens:** Do you want to specialize in roses, vegetables, perennials, annuals, shrubs, foliage plants, water gardening, rock gardening? You might want to mix some or all of these in one garden.
- **Features, structures, and furniture:** These can be nearly endless — fountains, statues, sculpture, bird feeder, decks, patios, paths, walls, berms, pergolas, trellises, gazebos, gazing globes, benches. Where will they be placed? What will they be made of? (This is a good time to remember that line between restraint and exuberance — don't overdo the garden decorations!)
- **Continuing satisfaction:** Will your garden be productive and attractive throughout the year? Read on!

Planning for Winter Interest

As you draw up your plan, whether for a new garden or for a renovation, you'll be deciding how much lawn you want, where trees and tall shrubs should be placed, where the vegetable and ornamental gardens will be located. Once you've done this, pretend that no season other than winter exists. What will keep you interested in your garden? What will keep you looking at it and deriving pleasure from it?

One source of pleasure will be the shapes and textures of the plantings in your garden; another will be wildlife, especially birds. Many plants may scarcely be noticed in spring and summer when they provide the background against which showy annuals and perennials dazzle our eyes. In the winter, however, these background plants — usually shrubs, trees, and vines — take on a featured role because of their bark, berries, and shapes. Views that were hidden by foliage during the growing months suddenly burst into prominence.

Here are some plants that will bring interest to your garden in the winter.

Barberry (Berberis)

Japanese barberry (B. thunbergii) reaches a height of about 1.5 m (5 feet) and produces small white flowers in spring. In the winter, its red berries last longer than those of any other shrub. It grows in any type of soil, endures deep shade, and is dependable even in the worst situations. Attracts cedar waxwings. To Zone 5.

Nature can give you a helping hand in surprising ways.

Cotoneaster shows nicely against these paving stones, which warm up on sunny winter days.

Cotoneaster gives pleasure throughout the year, as this early-autumn scene illustrates.

The winter sun plays up the colour and texture of birch bark.

ABOVE RIGHT:
The arching sprays of barberry would earn it a place in the winter garden even if it didn't hold its berries well.

Birch *(Betula)*

One of the most attractive trees no matter what the time of year, birch grows very quickly, can be planted near your house, and is wonderfully cold-hardy. Expect it to live about twenty-five years. In winter its white bark shows well against evergreens. Unfortunately, birches are susceptible to the bronze birch borer, especially in the milder zones (anything warmer than Zone 4). Attracts chickadees, finches, nuthatches, woodpeckers.

Paper birch (*B. papyrifera*), a native Canadian tree, can climb to 15 m (50 feet) and is not as susceptible to borers. Its bark looks particularly attractive in winter, and with its several stems it can give the impression of a small grove. To Zone 2.

Young's weeping birch (*B. pendula* 'Youngii') has a weeping, or dome-shaped, growth, as the name might suggest. To Zone 2.

Bittersweet *(Celastrus scandens)*

This deciduous vine climbs by twining around a tree, trellis, or other support, and can become rampant. You'll need a male and female to be assured of getting the female to produce its bright orange-red berries, which are excellent for winter bouquets. Grows in sun or shade. To Zone 3.

Cotoneaster *(Cotoneaster)*

Cotoneasters are versatile plants, since they come in all heights, from the low ones described here to those that can reach 6 m (20 feet). With their red berries, they show well in winter.

Bearberry cotoneaster (*C. dammeri*) is a low-mounding evergreen. It doesn't like to be pruned, so give it space. Its bright-red berries contrast nicely with its glossy dark-green foliage. It likes full sun, is slow growing, and prefers neutral or alkaline soil. To Zone 3.

Rockspray (*C. horizontalis*) is deciduous in cold climates but semievergreen in milder ones. Its pink June flowers are followed by red fruits. To Zone 5.

Peking cotoneaster (*Cotoneaster acutifolia*) is a shrub-type cotoneaster that grows to 4 m (12 feet) and attracts grosbeaks and cedar waxwings. To Zone 2.

Dogwood in summer and winter — another example of a plant that is attractive in more than one season.

Dogwood (*Cornus*)

Dogwood is generally grown as a large shrub. Many species have lovely red, purple, or grey stems.

Flowering dogwood (*C. florida*) attracts birds with the shiny red berries it produces throughout fall and early winter. During a drought, it needs deep watering. It can grow to about 12 m (40 feet). To Zone 6.

Japanese dogwood (*C. kousa*) is a smaller dogwood 6 m (20 feet), with fleshy pink-red fruits and bushy growth. It likes the shade. To Zone 5.

Siberian dogwood (*Cornus alba* 'Sibirica') grows to 2.7 m (9 feet). Its coral-red bark looks wonderful against snow. Because it likes damp soil, it's suitable for planting on low land or near the edge of a pond or stream. To Zone 2.

Euonymus (*Euonymus*)

Euonymus is a wonderful addition to any garden, no matter what the season. If you're looking for a plant that has winter interest, be sure to get the evergreen type. Its shiny green leaves show well against white snow, and some varieties have interesting bark and berries.

It is not demanding in its soil requirements and will even grow in sandy soil, doesn't mind being exposed to wind and salt spray, and can survive hot summers. Plant in full sun or partial shade. The branches, when cut, make a nice contribution to an indoor winter display. Outside, on very cold days, its leaves tend to curl. Give it a north or east exposure to help keep the evergreen varieties green all winter, and

The winged euonymus, just before heading into winter (ABOVE) and in its summer foliage (RIGHT).

A mature firethorn makes its presence felt when the summer glory of the garden has faded.

Try winterberry in a large garden, especially if you're interested in attracting birds, who will feast on the berries.

pray for snow, which prevents winter burn (most euonymus will recover easily from winter burn). Depending on the variety, the plant can be left to sprawl as a ground cover or to climb, or you can prune it; the evergreen varieties make a nice winter hedge. Generally to Zone 5, except for winged euonymus.

E. alatus, also known as winged euonymus and burning bush, grows to at least 2 m (6$^{1}/_{2}$ feet). This is a deciduous form of euonymus, but its feature in the winter garden is its bark, which is "winged" — that is, it has corky fins, or wings, in vertical ridges along the plant's main stems. To Zone 3.

Wintercreeper (*E. fortunei*) has many cultivars. I have had several of these growing against a west-facing garage wall for ten years now and they have completely covered the wall. In my Zone 5 garden, they are extremely hardy and hold their glossy green foliage all winter. The deep-green leaves of 'Emerald Gaiety' are edged in white, and in the fall turn a pinky colour. 'Variegatus' has small, shiny, gold-and-silver leaves throughout the winter. The bright-orange fruits of *E. fortunei* 'Vegeta' (evergreen bittersweet) last through winter into spring and will attract birds. It's a vigorous semievergreen that can be trained as a vine or left unpruned. Grows in semishade and can reach 6 m (20 feet).

Firethorn (*Pyracantha coccinea*)

Firethorn grows to 2 m (6$^{1}/_{2}$ feet) and does best in a sheltered, but sunny, location. This shrub is rather insignificant for most of the year, until it produces its gorgeous orange-red berries that stay on the plant all winter. To Zone 5.

Holly (*Ilex*)

Holly can be more than just a Christmas decoration. Its shiny green leaves and red berries show well whether there's snow on the ground or a West Coast drizzle falling.

Holly is a slow grower and can be a bit difficult to establish. Plant it in sun or partial shade, in well-drained acid soil, and shelter it from the west wind. Keep it well watered and mulched with peat moss or pine needles the first two years. It makes a good hedge. Treat all hollies as evergreens and fertilize once a month in April, May, June, and July with water-soluble 30-10-10.

Holly plants are either male or female, so you need one of each to produce berries on the female plant — although one male will pollinate several female plants.

American holly (*I. opaca*) is mainly a West Coast plant, with red fruits, though some varieties have yellow berries. Its dense growth gives protection to birds in winter. It likes a well-drained, acid soil and can grow to 9 m (30 feet). To Zone 7.

Blue holly (*I. × meserveae*) is an evergreen shrub with dark blue-green leaves and bright-red berries. To Zone 4.

English holly (*I. aquifolium*) prefers sun or light shade and rich, moist acid soil, and will do best on the East or West Coast. This evergreen type has shiny dark-green leaves and red berries (like the American holly, some varieties have yellow berries) during the winter months and makes a good hedge. To Zone 6.

Winterberry, or black alder (*I. verticillata*), is a large can go to 4 m (13 feet) deciduous holly that needs acid soil, but will tolerate either swampy or dry soil conditions. Its bright-red berries, which attract many species of birds, cluster in threes on its green-purple stems. The leaves blacken and fall in the cold, but the berries hang on until March. To Zone 3.

Ivy *(Hedera)*

The ivies listed here offer many possibilities for use in the garden — both English ivy (evergreen) and Boston ivy (deciduous) can be used as climbing vines or as ground covers. They can be put to good service on steep slopes to help prevent erosion.

Baltic ivy (*H. baltica*) might need some winter protection from the wind in zones 5 and 6. It wants rich, moist soils, and prefers shade to strong sun. Its leaves are smaller than those of English ivy, and turn purplish in winter. To Zone 5.

Boston ivy (*Parthenocissus tricuspidata*) is a dense, quick-growing, self-clinging deciduous vine with scarlet autumn foliage. Its dark-blue fruit is hardly visible until its leaves fall. Birds may nest in its woody growth. To Zone 4.

English ivy (*H. helix*) is another ivy that may require some winter protection. It likes rich, moist soils and prefers shade to strong sun. It offers shelter to small birds in winter. To Zone 4.

The brick wall helps provide warmth for English ivy (LEFT), *which can find very cold winters stressful. Boston ivy* (ABOVE) *will lose its bright autumn leaves but can provide delicate shadows on the snow on sunny winter days.*

Mountain ash makes a nice accent, especially when it produces its bright berries in late summer. They will often remain on the tree throughout the winter.

RIGHT:

An appealing combination well into the winter is Japanese maple and a low-growing juniper. In the summer, the Japanese maple is dominant with its coppery-green colour. In the winter, the juniper takes over as the showpiece, aided by the shadow etchings of the bare branches on the snow.

Japanese Maple (*Acer palmatum* 'Atropurpureum')

In the winter garden, the shadows of this small tree's branches make delicate tracings on the snow. It is a lovely addition to the garden, offering changing leaf colour throughout the spring (burgundy) to the summer (green) to the fall (scarlet). Look for the many named varieties that have particular distinguishing features, such as deeply serrated leaves or a graceful weeping habit. These maples may need protecting from frost. To Zone 5.

Mountain Ash (*Sorbus*)

European mountain ash (*S. aucuparia*) is a handsome tree to grow for its bright-red to orange berries that appear in August and last to February. This variety has a rounded form, and reaches a height of 4.5 to 10.5 m (15 to 35 feet). It likes full sun and a well-drained soil. It can be struck by fire blight, recognizable by dead shoots and withered leaves with cankers at their base. Try to avoid this disease by not pruning the tree. Attracts cedar waxwings and grosbeaks. To Zone 3.

Oregon Grape (*Mahonia aquifolium*)

A shrub that might be mistaken for a holly, Oregon grape (also known as Canadian holly) is an evergreen except when grown at the limit of its zone. Give it winter protection from sun and wind by wrapping it in layers of burlap; in the spring, when its fragrant yellow blooms appear, prune any foliage that has been winter damaged. In the late fall and early winter it carries blue-black grapelike berries among its purplish leaves. To Zone 5.

Privet (*Ligustrum*)

Amur privet (*L. amurense*), when grown as a shrub, offers birds blue-black berries and winter protection in its twiggy branches. It's good for cities because it can withstand much abuse—sand, salt spray, smog, and high winds—and makes a great hedge. To Zone 5.

Golden privet (*L.* x *vicaryi*) is another good privet for hedging, and shares many of the same qualities as the amur privet, though it's not as hardy. Left unpruned, it will grow to 90 cm (3 feet). Zone 6.

Rugosa Rose (*Rosa rugosa*)

Most roses don't look up to much during the winter—they're usually swathed in burlap or protected by mounds of soil and compost. Here's an exception. Its main attraction in winter is its bright-red hips (fruit), which are rich in vitamin C, but it also provides winter protection for birds. It grows easily in almost any conditions, even near the seashore, and makes a good hedge. To Zone 2.

Snowberry (*Symphoricarpos albus laevigatus*)

There are many snowberry varieties available, but this native shrub of western Canada is particularly nice. It grows to about 1.5 m (5 feet), and in the fall and winter produces cherry-sized white berries that attract birds. Plant it in front of evergreens or other tall plants, where its berries will be shown to advantage. It doesn't mind shade, adapts to all soils, and needs only average moisture. To Zone 2.

Sumac (*Rhus*)

Sumacs are deciduous shrubs that spread fairly quickly by means of suckers, so give them room.

Wild, or staghorn, sumac (*R. typhina*) produces rich red fruit clusters that last throughout the winter and attract birds. It's not fussy about soil type. To Zone 3.

Viburnum (*Viburnum*)

Viburnums are easy to grow—and give satisfaction year-round. Some are partially evergreen and will provide winter interest; most produce berries in the fall, though some varieties will hold their berries into the winter. They like full sun, but will grow in partial shade. Give these shrubs average, well-drained soil and a good drink late in the fall. (Viburnums have shallow roots and cannot take up moisture from the frozen ground during the winter.)

Birds are attracted to the berries of the viburnum. Depending on the variety (and there are many), they will grow to Zone 2, except as noted.

The delicate flowers of the Rugosa rose are replaced by showy hips in the winter.

A rewarding plant at any season, the Oregon grape carries these grapelike berries in winter.

European cranberry bush (*V. opulus*) is deciduous, with leaves that turn a rich red in the fall. The glossy berries are long-lasting, and become transparent as winter progresses. This species, which can grow to 3.6 m (12 feet), will tolerate wet or boggy soil. To Zone 3.

Highbush cranberry (*V. trilobum*) is a shade-tolerant shrub that reaches 3 m (10 feet). Its edible cherry-red fruit will hang on the branches until spring—although, since at least thirty-four species of birds compete for these delicacies, it's unlikely any will remain that long. To Zone 2.

V. tinus is an evergreen shrub with dark, glossy leaves, and grows up to 3 m (10 feet). The white flowers are followed by deep-blue small berries. To ensure fruiting, plant two or more specimens together. The buds start to open in November and continue throughout the winter during mild spells. This variety makes a good informal hedge or screen and is resistant to salt spray. To Zone 8.

Virginia Creeper (*Parthenocissus quinquefolia*)

The green foliage of this partially self-clinging, quickly growing vine turns a stunning red in the fall. Its blue-black berries, which are attractive to birds, hang on until the early winter. To Zone 2.

Winter Honeysuckle (*Lonicera fragrantissima*)

In milder zones, expect blooms as early as February; otherwise, you'll have to wait until March or April. In the colder zones, you can bring some branches inside for forcing. It makes a good hedge and can be pruned heavily. To Zone 5.

Winter Jasmine (*Jasminum nudiflorum*)

Allow winter jasmine to grow on a trellis or arbour, or train it against a fence or wall. In the milder regions of the country, it is covered with sunny yellow blossoms from December to March. Plant it in full sun, in a sheltered, well-drained spot. To Zone 5, but can't be depended on to flower in climates harsher than Zone 7.

Wintergreen (*Gaultheria procumbens*)

Wintergreen bears bright-red autumn fruit. Its small, dark, glossy leaves turn bronze and red in winter. Use it as a ground cover in shady areas. It will grow to a height of 60 cm (2 feet). To Zone 3.

Witch Hazel (*Hamamelis*)

In midwinter, witch hazel produces fragrant spidery blooms in shades of yellow, orange, gold, and red. This shrub likes good drainage, slightly acid soil, and full sun.

Chinese witch hazel (*H. mollis*) is a neat rounded deciduous shrub that produces fragrant yellow flowers in January and February in the mildest zones, and in early spring in colder zones; the flowers roll up in very cold spells. Bring its sweet-smelling blossoms indoors in the winter for a lovely perfume. To Zone 5.

Spring witch hazel (*H. vernalis*) produces small red to yellow fragrant flowers on mild days in January and February if it's planted in a well-protected spot. The flowers close on very cold days. To Zone 4.

Summer-flowering plants can add winter interest to the garden if seed heads and berries are left to overwinter.

Green in Winter

If you have any doubt about the vast array of greens nature provides, just take a look at evergreens in winter. Even within the juniper family, for example, colours range from subtle grey-greens to bright blues to bronzes and golds. Here is a small sampling of evergreens to give you an idea of the colours and shapes available as you plan your garden.

Cedars *(Thuja)*

Little Giant globe cedar (*Thuja occidentalis* 'Little Giant') and Rheingold cedar (*Thuja occidentalis* 'Rheingold') are both dwarf globe varieties. Little Giant is compact and bright-green, and needs no pruning. Rheingold is a copper-bronze in winter and needs full sun. Both grow to about 90 cm to 1.2 m (3 to 4 feet) and are hardy to Zone 3.

Juniper *(Juniperus)*

For a conical juniper, try *J. virginiana* 'Canaertii.' It has rich green foliage that must be sheared every year to maintain the conical form. It's a dwarf, reaching 1.5 m (5 feet). Some spreading junipers are *J. horizontalis* 'Plumosa Compacta,' whose feathery foliage turns from green in summer to rich plum in the winter; Tamarix juniper (*J. sabina* 'Tamariscifolia'), which has silvery green foliage; and blue rug juniper (*J. horizontalis* 'Wiltonii'), a popular low spreader with silver-blue foliage that looks fantastic in rock gardens or cascading over a retaining wall. All to Zone 2.

Pine *(Pinus)*

Limber pine (*P. flexilis*), available in western Canada only, grows very slowly to a mature height of 7 m (23 feet). It has dark-green to blue-green needles that give it soft look. Its branches are quite flexible, so that it can withstand heavy winds and snow loads. To Zone 3.

Swiss stone pine (*P. cembra*) is a slow-growing dwarf pine with a narrow pyramidal shape that becomes more open as the tree ages. Because it will be only 2 m (6½ feet) by its tenth year, it makes a good addition to an urban garden (it can eventually reach 9 m/30 feet). Its needles give a dark blue-green effect. Give it moist, acid, well-drained soil. To Zone 2.

Spruce *(Picea)*

Colorado spruce (*P. pungens*) has a variety of cultivars suitable for small gardens: Columnar blue spruce (*P. pungens glauca* 'Fastigata') has a narrow columnar shape with bright-blue foliage, and grows to 3 m (10 feet); Fat Albert spruce (*P. pungens glauca* 'Fat Albert') also grows to 3 m (10 feet), but is dense and has a pyramidal shape with blue foliage; Hoopsii blue spruce (*P. pungens* 'Hoopsii') grows to 10 m (33 feet) and has an intense silver-blue colour. All to Zone 2.

Yew *(Taxus)*

If you were so inclined, you could probably do all your shopping for evergreens from the wide selection of yews. Japanese yew (*T. cuspidata*) has shiny dark-green foliage and can be pruned to any height, but will grow to 3.6 to 6 m (12 to 20 feet). It has a soft texture and a pyramidal shape. To Zone 4. Hick's yew (*T. media* 'Hicksii') has a columnar shape, dark-green foliage, and red fruit in the fall. It will reach from 1.2 to 3 m (4 to 10 feet) and does well in a northern exposure. To Zone 5. Hunnewell yew (*T. intermedia* 'Hunnewelliana') is a shade-tolerant, low globe-shaped yew that responds well to clipping. To Zone 4.

Shapes and line become important in the winter. Here are some examples that provide a vertical line: Oriental cedar on the left, and an upright juniper on the right.

Attracting Birds

Birds and gardens seem made for each other, and one of the great pleasures of the garden in winter is the colour, movement, and interest that birds provide. The surest way to have birds in your garden is to feed them. But feeding the birds is a commitment; once you start, you should keep it up, at least for the winter.

Even the smallest garden can accommodate a freestanding bird feeder; apartment dwellers also should be able to find one to suit their conditions. Many commercial feeders are squirrel-proof (not that squirrels don't deserve food — they just shouldn't take it from the birds!), but be sure to situate where cats won't be able to prey on the birds.

Place the feeder close enough to the house that you can enjoy the birds and also see when the food is getting low. As well, you don't want to have to make a long trek through deep snow to fill it. Some birds like to feed on the ground and their needs are met by the seeds that get scattered by the birds at the feeder. Check out the Kids' Gardening section at the end of this chapter — it has more on feeding birds.

Water is important for birds, both for drinking and for bathing, which helps them keep their insulating feathers in good shape. So that the birds are supplied with fresh water in winter, replenish the container every day. Many stores that carry bird-feeding supplies also carry small heaters for keeping the water container free from ice. If you have an outdoor supply of electricity, bear this in mind as you plan the placement of your bird feeder and watering station.

Chickadees are entertaining visitors to the garden and are easy to attract in the winter.

When you're tidying up the garden in the fall, don't be too quick to get rid of all the stalks that have seed heads or berries. The birds will be attracted to the remains of plants such as cosmos, monarda, rudbeckia, or sunflowers.

The Productive Garden

Up to now, I've been concentrating on the ornamental garden in my discussion of planning and design. Let's look at the vegetable garden, a spot that offers many possibilities for lengthening the gardening season and practising techniques for bumper crops — to suit bumper appetites.

Renewing the vegetable garden: Because the plants in a vegetable garden are usually annuals (asparagus and berry plants are exceptions), you'll be renewing, rather than renovating, your vegetable garden each year. But as you mull over your plans for your new or renovated garden, make sure that your vegetable patch is in the best spot. Does it warm up quickly in the spring and hold the warmth in the fall? Would raised beds be a good idea (see Chapter 3 for information about raised beds)? If you haven't got that wonderful season extender, the cold frame, in your garden, make room for one in your design.

The Cold Frame

First of all, "cold frame" is a misnomer. This all-important tool is the most versatile season extender you're likely to find. Because of the way it's used (to warm soil, protect plants, and insulate both), it's really a warm frame! The only thing cold about it is the temperature on the outside during those early-spring and late-fall days in Canada.

Many gardeners use cold frames extensively in the spring to get a head start with seedlings, but these minigreenhouses can help you keep harvesting well into the winter, not only in the milder parts of the country but in the colder ones, too.

As we work our way through the gardening year, I'll include suggestions about using the cold frame to help extend your growing season. I'm introducing you to the cold frame in January because this is your planning month. You can work into your garden plans the site for a permanent cold frame for starting seedlings or hardening off, or decide to use a movable one in various parts of the garden to protect tender plants.

A cold frame is a bottomless box with a frame and lid, which serves as a small greenhouse for plants. The frame can be constructed of materials such as wood, metal, concrete, brick, or even bales of hay. The hinged cover is made of clear plastic or glass (old storm windows are often used as covers). The cold frame has sloping sides — it's higher at the back than at the front — so that the cover rests at an angle to make the most of the sun's rays. Because it's bottomless, it sits directly on the ground or can be sunk a few centimetres into the ground. Preferably, it faces due south, with the long edge on the east-west axis; west- or east-facing cold frames can provide adequate shelter, as well. The ideal position for a cold frame is against a south-facing wall of a house, where the heat reflected from the house will help warm the frame. Unfortunately, cold frames are usually not especially attractive, so you may not want

A bat house like this is not often seen in gardens, but these nocturnal flyers will help keep insects in check. The opening is at the bottom — the bat flies in and hangs upside down in the box.

yours near your house, but the closer your frame is, the more likely you are to use it during the cold months.

If you're handy, January or February are good times to build this versatile gardening aid. Make it to any dimensions you desire, but a good size to start with is 60 cm (2 feet) high at the back, 30 cm (1 foot) high at the front, and 60 cm (2 feet) from front to back. This measurement from front to back should not be greater than your reach, so that you have easy access to all the plants. The slope of the sides is between 2.5 cm (1 inch) and 5 cm (2 inches) for every 30 cm (1 foot) from back to front. The length will be dictated by the type of covering you use — for example, if you use old storm windows, the length will be based on the width of the windows. I'm sure that as you find more and more uses for your cold frame, you will want a larger one. An advantage of larger frames is that they maintain a more consistent and higher temperature for longer.

The front edge of the cover should overhang the front of the frame to let rain and snow drain off easily. Add extra rigid insulation on the inside of the frame for the winter months (see instructions on insulating the cold frame, which follow); otherwise, use old blankets, sheets, or curtains to retain warmth and to protect the plants from the stressful freeze-thaw-freeze cycles that make our winters unpredictable.

Lightweight aluminum cold frames are quite versatile; you can move them around the garden to cover particular plants and to take advantage of sun or shade. However, one benefit of having the frame in a permanent place is that the soil it sits on can easily be enriched with compost and other fertilizers.

If the soil in the permanent cold-frame site is healthy and productive, just dig and nourish the ground as you would for a regular bed. If the soil is heavy, dig and turn the earth, removing any sod or stones. Work in some topsoil and compost and any other fertilizer you wish, such as composted manure.

Uses for the Cold Frame

Winter
- To harvest food plants that were planted out earlier in the season.
- To plant new crops for winter and early-spring harvesting.
- To contain overwintered crops for harvesting in the spring.

Spring
- To harden off seedlings started indoors in winter.
- To sow seeds for transplanting. (Plants started in a cold frame tend to be quite hardy — they've already been exposed to fluctuating temperatures, and can often be planted straight into the garden once conditions are appropriate.)
- To protect tender seedlings from frost.

Summer
- To use as a "nursery" for ailing plants.
- To start seedlings for fall plantings.

Fall
- To lengthen the growing season of late-summer and early-fall plantings of leafy crops.
- To protect late-season crops from frost.
- To keep cuttings of hardy shrubs and perennials to be planted out in the spring.
- To hold divided perennials for spring planting.

Homemade cold frame designs are limited only by a gardener's ingenuity and the available materials. Although there are many commercial cold frames on the market, homemade efforts are no less productive. You don't need a lot of space, but the smaller they are, the sooner they will cool off, thus limiting their usefulness.

The Insulated Frame

A good way to get more use out of a cold frame is by insulating the sides and back and installing rigid insulation that extends below the frost line. In order to make the maximum use of the sun's rays, the back wall (the north wall) should be quite high; the front wall (the south) will be low — perhaps no more than 15 cm (6 inches). The important calculation is the angle needed for the cover — it's easy to figure out: your latitude plus ten degrees. The farther north you are, the higher the latitude and the steeper the slope of the cover. For example, Toronto's latitude is close to forty-four degrees, so the optimum angle would be fifty-four degrees; Winnipeg's latitude is fifty degrees, so the angle for the cover would be sixty degrees. As the angle becomes steeper, you might want to make a narrow roof of the same material as the sides.

The ideal location for an insulated frame is also against the south wall of a house (again, you're more likely to use it during the winter if it's accessible). Otherwise, any spot that will get the winter sun and be fairly well sheltered from winter winds will do. Dig a pit 60 cm (2 feet) deep to the outside dimensions of your planned frame. Set the soil aside, keeping the subsoil and the topsoil separate. Place 5 cm (2 inches) of rigid insulation in the bottom and sides of the pit so that the side insulation extends 5 cm (2 inches) above the ground level. Put the subsoil back in the pit, then the topsoil. Add compost, leaf mould, or composted manure to the topsoil to enrich your growing medium. Construct the frame as for a normal cold frame, but insulate the back and sides. Caulk all joints. The cover should be double glazed. You could

Look around your property — you might be able to claim a corner for a lean-to greenhouse. This one offers more flexibility and ease of use than a cold frame would in the same area.

also make a separate cover of the rigid insulation, to be used at night to help conserve the warmth built up over the day. The smaller the frame, the more quickly it will lose heat during the night.

Ventilation can be extremely important in such an airtight structure. The insulated frame will be closed most of the time during the winter, except when you open it to harvest a crop. Let some fresh air into the frame by opening the cover a few centimetres whenever daytime temperatures rise above freezing.

Watering should be minimal, because the atmosphere inside the frame will be kept moist by the water given off by the plants themselves. Keep an eye out for aphids and spray with insecticidal soap the moment you spot any.

Successfully using an insulated cold frame throughout the winter may not be possible in many regions of Canada, but it can certainly help extend the gardening season.

Using the Cold Frame in Winter

The way you use your cold frame will vary from season to season, perhaps even within a season. It's likely the plants that are in the cold frame during the deepest part of the winter are just waiting for you to harvest them. They've already done their growing, so light is not absolutely essential. Snowfalls that blanket your frame cut the light off, but also act as an insulator, so you won't harm your plants if you leave the snow on the frame.

If your plants are just waiting for harvesting—that is, they're dormant—adding moisture is not necessary.

Experiment with different ways of maintaining heat in the frame if the plants you've got in there won't tolerate extremely low temperatures. Dark-painted rocks can store the heat of the sun, to be released during the night. Digging "hot" (fresh) manure into the soil of the cold frame is a time-honoured way of warming the frame. Any kind—cattle, sheep, horse, or chicken—will do; just be sure to cover it with 5 to 10 cm (2 to 4 inches) of soil. Of course, tucking the cold frame in at night with old blankets or bedspreads, for example, will also help. Without these aids, the temperature in your cold frame may occasionally drop below the freezing point. This won't mean that you've lost your crops. Wait until any frozen plant material has thawed before harvesting—and don't dawdle as you get it into the house! If the outer leaves of crops such as radicchio or spinach are mushy because of a freeze-thaw-freeze cycle in the frame, just peel them away and harvest the leaves closer to the centre.

The Collapsible Cold Frame

Manufacturers of cold frames are responding to the needs of gardeners and producing collapsible cold frames that take up very little space. Some models have as many as three vertical tiers, and are upright, rather than low to the ground. They'd work well for a balcony, a small patio, or a modest urban garden.

Kids' Gardening:
Feeding the Birds

Involve your kids in your winter garden by showing them how easy it is to make treats for the birds.

Bird Feeders

Some feeders can be made from "found" objects such as orange crates, milk cartons, and plastic bottles. To make a feeder from a milk carton, cut off the front part to about 2.5 cm (1 inch) above the bottom. Angle the cut in from the top to the bottom and make a perch by threading a small piece of dowelling through the lip that remains.

Well-scrubbed bottles, such as plastic bleach bottles or pop bottles, can easily be turned into bird feeders. Just cut out a large opening on one side of the bottle (leave enough of the bottle to provide protection for the food). Put a hole in the cap and string some strong twine through it, screw the top back on the bottle, and there you have it—an easy-to-make bird feeder.

The Food

Suet—white beef fat—is a good source of energy for birds and plays an important role in the recipes for homemade bird feed.

You can use the suet as is, putting it in a mesh bag such as an onion bag, tying it securely at the open end, and hanging it from a tree or a hook attached to a wooden bird feeder. You can also melt the suet to mix it with other ingredients or to pour it into containers that can be set on feeder trays.

Suet seed mix: Melt at least 225 g (1/2 pound) of suet in the top of a double boiler. Add peanuts, seeds (such as millet, wheat, crushed corn, buckwheat, sunflower seeds, oats, rapeseed), raisins and currants, and peanut butter. Make the total volume of all the additions about equal to the volume of the suet. When the mixture has hardened, scrape it into mesh bags, or use it in some of the projects that follow. A bizarre-sounding treat—to humans, anyway—is suet mixture to which dead houseflies have been added. The birds love it!

Suet log: Adults will have to help kids make this feeder. Take a log of cedar, fir, poplar, or birch about 8 to 10 cm (3 to 4 inches) in diameter and 36 to 46 cm (14 to 18 inches) long. Drill holes 2.5 to 4 cm (1 to 1 1/2 inches) deep and 3.2 to 4 cm (1 1/4 to 1 1/2 inches) in diameter at various spots around the log; you can probably get four or five holes in a log of this size. Fill these holes with melted suet. Insert an eye hook at one end and hang the log in a tree.

Birds' buffet: Use suet, the suet seed mix, or a mixture of nuts and seeds to fill empty grapefruit halves and coconut shells. Cut an end off the coconut and drill three small holes, equally spaced, just below the rim. Thread strong twine through the holes and hang the feeder from a branch or a plant hanger on the deck.

Peanut-butter cones: Fat pine cones are easy to fill with peanut butter or a mixture of peanut butter and suet. Hang them outside.

Citrus rind: Baltimore orioles and buntings will enjoy this delicacy in the spring. Nail the rind to the top of a post.

January Gardening Checklist

The timing of the activities in the checklists should be regarded as a guideline. As you plan your gardening chores, take into account the conditions in your area, checking your first and last frost dates while planning when to start seeds indoors, when to set out seedlings, and when to sow seeds outdoors.

General

- Draw up garden plan; if garden is established, note any changes you want to make this year.
- Order seeds and plants from catalogues. Look for vegetable varieties that have an early harvest. When seeds arrive, arrange packets by seeding dates.
- Build a cold frame.
- Inspect garden tools and sharpen, clean, or repair those in need of it.
- Clean houseplant foliage weekly to wash away spider mite or whitefly.
- Bring into the house branches of witch hazel, forsythia, pussy willow, euonymus, camellia, purple sand cherry, or serviceberry for forcing.
- Get ready for sowing seeds indoors by cleaning your pots, setting up a lighting system, and preparing labels.

Ornamental Garden

- Inspect stored bulbs, corms, and tubers. Discard any that are rotten.
- Sow geraniums under lights.
- Brush snow off evergreens to prevent branches from breaking.

Zones 2 to 6

- Add evergreen boughs to your roses for extra insulation, especially in a winter with little snow.
- From now until March there is always the danger of a mild spell followed by a freezing spell. Check mulch on all plants to be sure it hasn't been dislodged. If it has, replace it, tucking it firmly around and over the plant. Add more if necessary.
- Sow pansies for planting out in April. Sow snapdragons for planting out in May.

Zones 7 to 9

- Be ready to protect tender shrubs and perennials from ice and frost.
- Clean up flower beds and lawn, taking off leaves, twigs, broken stalks.
- Plant bare-root roses unless ground is frozen or water-logged.
- Turn the compost if weather allows.

Fruit and Vegetable Garden

Zones 2 to 6

- Prune fruit trees in mild weather (see Chapter 7 for pruning information).

Zones 7 to 9

- Protect tender herbs if weather is cold.
- Start lettuce and other cool-weather greens in the cold frame. Sow beet seeds in the cold frame, as well.

Chapter 2

February

Hopes and Green Dreams

Rule of Thumb

Generally, if you buy your nursery stock locally it will be hardy in your zone. If in doubt, ask. If you order plants from nurseries in zones colder than yours, you should also be safe. Be cautious about ordering plant material from zones milder than yours.

Whether you live in the milder regions of the country, where snowdrops are already blooming, or in the coldest regions, where the snow is still sparkling under a bright-blue February sky, you're more aware of the lengthening days. The gardening spirit never hibernates, so you're eager to continue with garden plans and dreams. Pull out those catalogues you've been thumbing through and get ready to start ordering seeds.

As you flip through the pages of your seed catalogues, or when you're reading gardening books and magazines, you might find in their pages reproductions of hardiness-zone maps. Even if your catalogues don't have zone maps, you'll likely find designations such as "Hardy to Zone 4" attached to some of the descriptions of the plants. Understanding the basics of hardiness zones is important, especially if you want to extend the gardening season and obtain the best yield possible from your garden. Knowing about your zone will help you choose plants that will prosper in your garden, and save you from heartbreak. Of course, your garden might be a zone or even two warmer than the zone indicated on the map, so temper your knowledge of your "official" zone with what you know about your own garden as you choose plants.

Zone maps are at best imprecise, and even the experts disagree about the classification of the zones. As well, our climate is changing and average temperatures of even twenty years ago can differ from those of today.

Zones

Canada has been divided into ten climate regions called hardiness zones, starting with Zone 0, the coldest zone, in the Far North, and going up to Zone 9, the mildest. The hardiness map is a rough guide to your zone, especially if you live near the merging of two zones, and you need not follow it slavishly. Many gardeners push the limits of their zone or create a microclimate (more about that shortly) in their garden to widen the plant material that will survive there.

The Canadian system uses minimum temperatures to differentiate the zones, and takes into account a variety of other factors: the mean maximum temperature of the warmest month, the length of the frost-free period, the amount of rainfall from June to November, the depth of snow cover, and the wind speed. The most important elements of this mix are the temperature of the coldest month and the length of the growing season.

Snow may still be on the ground, but the sun carries the promise of warmer days ahead.

The carefree mix of annuals and perennials in this Maritimes garden shows what can be achieved by choosing plants that thrive in your zone.

You may be near the boundary of the next zone or your microclimate may be a zone warmer than the map says. So the best way to check on what's hardy in your area is to talk to other gardeners and people at your local horticultural society and garden centres. Nothing can replace local experience and observation. You can also figure out what zone you're in by looking for what are called indicator plants in your area (more about that shortly, too).

Here's a rundown of the zones in Canada and their average annual minimum temperatures.

Zone Minimum Temperatures

0 below -45°C (-50°F)
1 -45°C (-50°F)
2 -45 to -40°C (-50 to -40°F)
3 -40°C (-40°F)
4 -35 to -29°C (-30 to -20°F)

5 -29 to -23°C (-20 to -10°F)
6 -23 to -18°C (-10 to 0°F)
7 -18 to -12°C (5 to 10°F)
8 -12 to -7°C (10 to 20°F)
9 -7 to -1°C (20 to 30°F)

Microclimates

A microclimate can be thought of as a zone within a zone. Although your zone map may tell you that you are in Zone 5, your garden may rate at Zone 6 because of the moderating effect of hedges and trees, paved areas, buildings, soil type, elevation, proximity to a body of water, and many other factors. You can go to the trouble of keeping track of frost dates and minimum temperatures for several years to find out if your garden is in a different zone from the one the "experts" say, but the easiest way to decide on your zone is to see what grows in your neighbourhood. Gardening is a

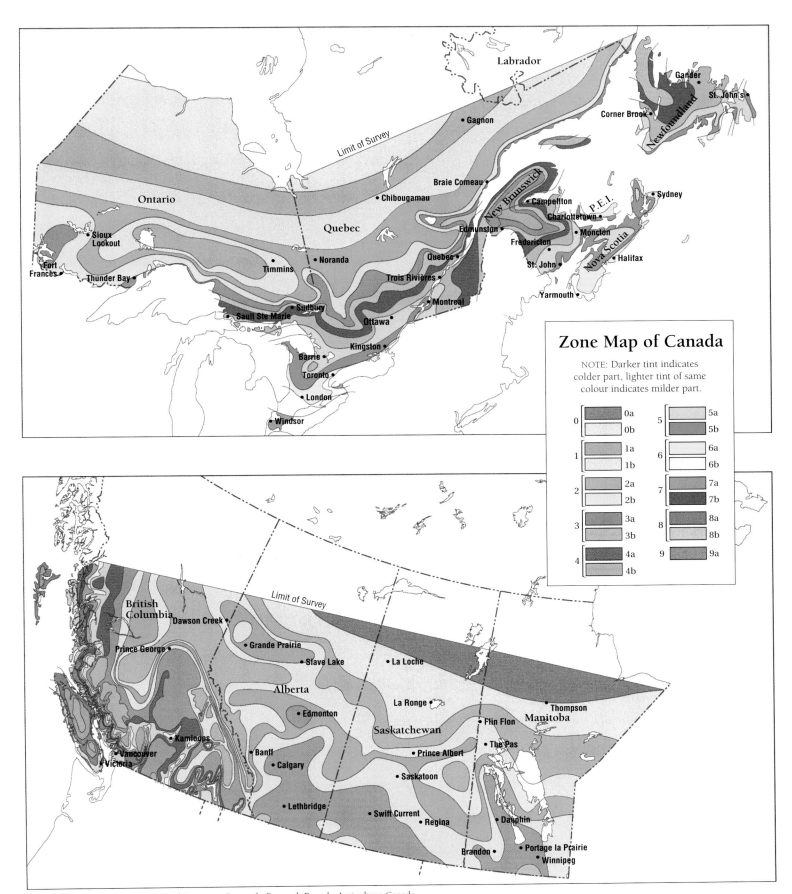

Zone Map of Canada

NOTE: Darker tint indicates colder part, lighter tint of same colour indicates milder part.

0	0a
	0b
1	1a
	1b
2	2a
	2b
3	3a
	3b
4	4a
	4b
5	5a
	5b
6	6a
	6b
7	7a
	7b
8	8a
	8b
9	9a

Source: Centre for Land and Biological Resources Research, Research Branch, Agriculture Canada

friendly pursuit — talk to your neighbours, peer into their gardens, wander the streets of your community, noting what's doing well and what isn't. If you're feeling adventurous, try a plant or two designated hardy only to a zone higher than yours — if you're in Zone 4, try some perennial flax, for example. It's considered hardy only to Zone 4, and if it fails, you won't have lost an expensive plant — just a very pretty one.

The ultimate in microclimates that I've seen is at a friend's house in Toronto. He grows figs by planting them against the outside of his chimney stack — with the heat of a continually burning wood stove and the protection of a burlap cover, he truly cheats on climate zones.

Plant Indicators*

This list will help you discover which zone you are in with more accuracy than the hardiness map. If the plants listed in each zone flourish in your area, you can be fairly certain of your hardiness zone. If all plants listed from zones 1 through 5 survive in your area, you live in Zone 5.

Zone 1: Saskatoonberry (*Amelanchier alnifolia*), hedge cotoneaster (*Cotoneaster lucida*), mugo pine (*Pinus mugo mughus*).

Zone 2: Siberian peashrub (*Caragana arborescens*), Siberian dogwood (*Cornus alba* 'Sibirica'), European cotoneaster (*Cotoneaster integerrima*).

Zone 3: Winged spindletree (*Euonymus alata*), staghorn sumac (*Rhus typhina*), garland spirea (*Spirea* x *arguta*).

Zone 4: Peegee hydrangea (*Hydrangea paniculata* 'Grandiflora'), mock orange (*Philadelphus* 'Bouquet Blanc'), Japanese yew (*Taxus cuspidata*).

Zone 5: Smokebush (*Cotinus coggygria*), early forsythia (*Forsythia ovata*), fragrant viburnum (*Viburnum carlesii*).

Zone 6: Japanese maple (*Acer palmatum*), slender deutzia (*Deutzia gracilis*), showy forsythia (*Forsythia* x *intermedia* 'Spectabilis').

Zone 7: English box (*Buxus sempervirens*), St.-John's-Wort (*Hypericum hookerianum* 'Hidcote'), cherry laurel (*Prunus laurocerasus*).

Zone 8: Japanese aucuba (*Aucuba japonica*), Chilean pernettya (*Pernettya mucronata*), laurustinus (*Viburnum tinus*).

Zone 9a: Plum cryptomeria (*Cryptomeria japonica* 'Elegans'), sweet bay or laurel (*Laurus nobilis*), Chinese pieris (*Pieris forrestii*).

With a basic understanding of zones and hardiness, you can begin to make lists of plants and seeds that you want to order for your garden.

Most vegetables are annuals, so knowing your zone isn't as important to vegetable growers. The important numbers are dates — the dates of the last and first frosts in your area. The zone map will help you figure this out to a certain degree, but close observation of your conditions is really the best way of determining when it's safe to plant tender vegetable seedlings outside and when you can expect a killing frost.

*Source: C. E. Ouellet and Lawrence C. Sherk, *Map of Plant Hardiness Zones in Canada* (Ottawa: Canada Dept. of Agriculture, 1967).

Scilla — one of the first blooms in the spring garden

City and Zone, with Average Last-Frost and Average First-Frost Dates

St. John's, Nfld. (5b)	June 1	Oct. 11	Winnipeg, Man. (3a)	May 23	Sept. 22
Charlottetown, P.E.I. (5b)	May 16	Oct. 15	Prince Albert, Sask. (1b)	June 1	Sept. 5
Halifax, N.S. (6a)	May 12	Oct. 15	Regina, Sask. (2b)	May 24	Sept. 11
Sydney, N.S. (5b)	May 23	Oct. 14	Saskatoon, Sask. (2b)	May 27	Sept. 14
Yarmouth, N.S. (6b)	May 2	Oct. 21	Beaver Lodge, Alta. (1b)	May 24	Sept. 7
Chatham, N.B. (5a)	May 19	Sept. 23	Calgary, Alta. (3a)	May 25	Sept. 15
Fredericton, N.B. (5a)	May 19	Sept. 23	Edmonton, Alta. (3a)	May 25	Sept. 8
Saint John, N.B. (5b)	May 16	Oct. 3	Kamloops, B.C. (6)	May 4	Oct. 1
Arvida, P.Q. (3b)	May 21	Sept. 20	Prince George, B.C. (3)	June 6	Aug. 31
Montreal, P.Q. (5b)	May 3	Oct. 8	Prince Rupert, B.C. (8)	May 11	Oct. 15
Quebec, P.Q. (4b)	May 13	Sept. 28	Vancouver, B.C. (8b)	March 31	Nov. 3
Sherbrooke, P.Q. (4a)	June 2	Sept. 10	Victoria, B.C. (8b/9a)	April 8	Oct. 29
Kapuskasing, Ont. (2a)	May 10	Sept. 2	Dawson, Yukon (0)	May 28	Aug. 28
London, Ont. (6b)	May 10	Oct. 5	Whitehorse, Yukon (0)	June 8	Aug. 30
Ottawa, Ont. (5a)	May 7	Oct. 2	Frobisher Bay, NWT (0)	June 28	Aug. 27
Thunder Bay, Ont. (3a)	May 30	Sept. 12	Inuvik, NWT (0)	June 23	Aug. 14
Toronto, Ont. (6b)	May 8	Oct. 5	Resolute, NWT (0)	July 10	July 20
Churchill, Man. (0a)	June 24	Sept. 9	Yellowknife, NWT (0)	May 27	Sept. 16
The Pas, Man. (1b)	May 24	Sept. 17			

Counting the days between the last and first frosts will give you the number of frost-free days in your area. If you don't know your last frost date, call your local Department of Agriculture branch or garden centre.

Season Extenders

As you mull over your garden plans, you can incorporate a few features to help warm up your garden no matter what the zone, thus extending both the growing season and the range of plants you can choose from.

- If you have a hilly plot, consider planting your garden on a south-facing hill. Your plants will suffer less frost damage than if planted in a low-lying site or on a north-facing hill. On the other hand, if your hill is fairly exposed, your plants could suffer wind damage even on the south side. You could plant evergreens as windbreaks, however, to break cold north and east winds. Don't put in a windbreak below any sloping area you will be planting because it will impede the downward flow of the cool air and hold it over your garden.
- The soil in raised beds warms up more quickly in the spring than the soil in beds at the normal level. Raised beds also provide good drainage, let you make the best and richest soil possible without a lot of digging, and allow you to garden more intensively in a smaller space. For more about raised beds, see Chapter 3.
- Climbing plants will bear fruit earlier when trained up a trellis, where they can catch the sun.
- Make a spot that will warm up early in the spring by building a brick or stone wall to enclose a south-facing spot. Spring bulbs planted in such a corner will bloom early and can make it a pleasant place to sit on a sunny spring day.
- Installing a permanent cold frame (discussed in Chapter 1) will give you a sheltered place to harden off seedlings and overwinter half-hardy plants.

Indoor Plants

By February, you might start looking at your indoor plants with a more critical eye. The plants have come through the deepest winter, with the lowest light, and are now ready to get growing more vigorously! This is a perfect time to help them get ready for spring, before you're busy with all the jobs that need to be done outdoors.

Now is when you should practise preventive medicine on your plants, pruning, trimming, and repotting them. The soil mix you use will be important, because they need nutrients to help them put on their spring and summer growth.

Minor surgery: Whether it's a vigorous Swedish ivy indoors or a sturdy climbing hydrangea outdoors, most people have great trouble with the idea of cutting anything away from their living plants. Many gardeners don't seem bothered by the minor grooming of plants, picking off dead leaves and spent flowers, but taking scissors or secateurs in hand appear to cause panic. Fear not — you're doing them a favour. Cutting away not just old growth but healthy new branches can actually help your indoor plants to be more attractive and to flourish.

First, get rid of all dead and dying leaves and stems on your indoor plants. Leaving them on can attract fungal infections; cutting them off will encourage healthy new growth. Aim to trim the plant so it retains its shape and is not lopsided. Observe the plant from several angles before you commit yourself to the first cuts. Have a look at the plant in garden centres, public greenhouses, or books to see what its natural shape is, then try to maintain that as you prune.

Pinching back

Prune plants with strong stems using scissors or secateurs.

Use small pruning scissors, and have a small sharp knife close by. Remove leaves and stems with the scissors and small branches and woody growth with the knife; cut to just above a leaf bud that points in the direction you want the new growth to go. If it's a plant with many branches, make sure the middle of the plant is not too dense with competing branches. Start by getting rid of the weaker competing branches. Once you've done the pruning and seen the good results, you'll lose your fear of it.

Pinching: Throughout the year, you'll be practising another kind of pruning: pinching. By pinching back growth, you can encourage your plants to become fuller, bushier, and more attractive; if they produce flowers, you'll be rewarded with larger blooms. When you pinch plants, use your thumbnail and index finger to make a clean break in the leaves, buds, or stems you're taking off. You'll usually be taking off less than 2.5 cm (1 inch) when you're pinching—anything bigger probably requires scissors or a knife.

Some people are intimidated by pinching, but whenever you snip off a cutting to give to a friend, remind yourself that this is a form of pinching. As well, I find pinching back plants is great way to relax and gives me an opportunity to inspect plants for tiny unwelcome visitors.

Repotting: Indoor plants in small pots can use up the soil nutrients in less than a year. Even feeding the plants additional nutrients throughout the year will not sustain the plant forever; insoluble salts in the fertilizer can build to toxic levels; these salts appear as a powdery white residue on the pot. So give your plants a break—and some new soil. You might want to provide your plant with a new pot if the old one has become discoloured because of the buildup of salts. Let new clay pots soak in water for several hours and then dry before using. If you are using the old pot, clean it well before repotting.

The salt building up on this pot needs to be cleaned before the Kalanchoe begins to suffer.

Make sure the soil in the old pot is fairly dry before you repot. If you're using a new pot, choose one with a hole in the bottom. Place a screen over the hole to prevent the soil from washing out. To help keep the soil sweet, add about 15 mL (1 tablespoon) of horticultural charcoal for a small pot or 30 mL (2 tablespoons) for a larger pot. Put some of your new potting soil in the pot.

Cover the drainage hole of a clean pot as you prepare to repot a plant.

Use potting soil specially formulated for household plants.

Carefully remove the plant from the old pot. It's easiest if the soil has been allowed to dry out.

After removing some of the old soil, lower the plant into the new pot. The "collar" should sit about 1.25 cm (1/2 inch) below the rim, so add soil as necessary.

Remove the plant from its old pot. You might have to knock the pot gently against a hard surface to release the root ball. Holding the pot with one hand, carefully grasp the plant close to the soil with the other and wiggle it out of the pot. With the plant released, remove as much of the old soil as possible. You can even cut off some of the roots. It's safe to remove as much as a third of the root mass — it's a form of pruning that will benefit the plant over time.

Place the plant in the centre of the pot so that its "collar" (where the plant material meets the soil) is about 1.25 cm (1/2 inch) below the rim. You may have to lift out the plant several times to get it at the right depth. Once you're satisfied with the depth, start filling in the rest of the space with soil, patting it in place with your fingers or thumbs as you go. You don't want to compact the soil, but you do want to be sure that all air pockets have been eliminated. Finally, tap the pot on your work surface for a final settling of the soil and thoroughly water the plant with 5-15-5 transplanter solution to help establish new roots quickly.

The plant should not go immediately to a sunny window, but should recuperate in a bright area, away from direct sunlight. If it seems to be struggling after a few days, make a minigreenhouse for it with a clear plastic bag, but do not seal the bag for more than forty-eight hours or disease spores will begin to multiply.

Tips for Houseplant Care

Now that you know about caring for your houseplants in the winter, let's look at some tips for keeping them healthy year-round.

Soil: Using the soil from outdoors can introduce diseases and pests to your indoor plants, so play it safe and purchase commercial potting soil specially mixed for houseplants. You'll be sure of getting a clean-growing medium for your plants. If you feel the need, you can add a small amount of purchased compost to the soil to enrich it.

The soil should be porous so that the roots can spread easily and so that water will be quickly and thoroughly absorbed by it.

Light and temperature: Many houseplants thrive in the regular sunlight that comes through windows; some require special grow lights. Some plants (bird's nest fern, for example) prefer an east light, while some (spathe flower, for example) like the west; some plants want filtered light (wandering Jew) and others are quite adaptable—the hoya does best in four hours of direct sun daily but will also do quite well in bright indirect light. There are some "industrial-strength" plants out there that seem to survive under the most adverse conditions. Do a bit of research into what your particular plant's needs are.

If temperature is ever a problem for houseplants in the winter, it's usually a case of the temperature being too high, rather than too low. Many houseplants prefer it a bit on the cool side, especially at night. Because our homes are so well heated in winter, they often are very dry—that's more of a problem for plants than light or temperature. The humidity in the average Canadian home in the winter is in the range of 12 to 15 percent. Compare that with the Sahara Desert at 24 percent and you *know* our homes are dry! Installing a humidifier will be beneficial to your plants' health, as well as your own.

Watering: As with light, plants' needs differ, but there are a few tips that apply to all plants. It's best to water your houseplants with room-temperature water; cold water can shock the roots and they won't absorb the moisture as easily as warmer water. Also, most municipalities add chlorine and fluoride to the water that comes out of our taps. It's a good idea to let this tap water sit overnight to allow these gases to escape, before using it on your plants.

To see if your plant needs watering, push your finger gently into the soil. If the soil gives a bit, don't water. If the soil feels dry and is unyielding, it's time to water. Water the plants well—give them a good soaking, until the water drains out the bottom of the pot. Throw that excess away, water again, and remove any excess from the second watering.

How often do plants need watering? Although it's easier for us humans to have a schedule for watering our plants, the plants might not need to be watered at the same time every week; in fact, their watering requirements change throughout the year. Research your plants and get to know their needs. Generally, during the winter months they will need less watering; although the atmosphere in your house is likely to be dry because of central heating, the plants' growth is very slow in the winter.

Some plants benefit from a light misting of water on their leaves. Above is one of many types of misters that are available.

In my experience, nine times out of ten, houseplants die from overwatering rather than underwatering, so err on the side of caution. Overwatering causes the soil to become compacted and the roots to become waterlogged, so that they cannot absorb the oxygen they need.

Feeding: Your houseplants may flourish with no extra nutrient feeding, but if your plant has special needs or is looking a bit down at the heel, there are dozens of fertilizers and plant foods available. Read their labels carefully and get to know what the numbers mean (see Chapter 3 for a full discussion of those numbers). Always use the fertilizer in moderation — more is definitely not better — and apply it when the soil is moist.

See Chapter 11 for a list of some of my favourite houseplants, with notes for their care.

Herbs Indoors

Fresh basil for pesto in February; fresh parsley, sage, and thyme for the Christmas-turkey stuffing; fresh rosemary for lamb stew, with fresh snipped chives sprinkled over mashed potatoes in January — what could be better? It's not hard to have these treats if you keep in mind a few tips about growing herbs indoors.

- Herbs will do best in a south-facing window where they will receive at least six hours of sunlight. Otherwise, provide them with supplemental lighting.
- Cool temperatures will give you the best growth.
- In general, let the top 2.5 cm (1 inch) of soil get dry between waterings. I've noted any herbs that need watering more frequently. Make sure the pot has a hole in the bottom for good drainage. Wash the foliage when you water.
- Herbs prefer high humidity. Provide this by setting the pots on a bed of pebbles in a tray. Keep the water level in the tray just up to the top of the pebbles but not touching the pots.
- Use your herbs frequently — cutting them back encourages them to put on new growth and will give them a tidy shape.

Here are some basic, easy-to-grow herbs I wouldn't be without in the winter.

Basil (*Ocimum basilicum*)

Basil's green leaves have a warm spicy taste that goes well with tomatoes, but toss it into any soup, stew, or salad for extra taste. The youngest leaves give the nicest flavours. Don't entirely strip a stem when you're taking leaves — keep at least two leaves on a stem to encourage more growth. Feed with a weak fish emulsion once or twice a month. Basil might need to be watered more frequently than some other herbs. Spray it with water once a week to keep it free of insects.

Bay (*Laurus*)

Snip off a shiny stiff green leaf as a tasty addition to meat dishes, soups, and sauces. Bay can be grown to a bush or small tree and takes well to pruning to give it a nice shape. It prefers a cool location.

Herbs are fragrant, attractive, and edible and can easily be grown indoors with sufficient light. Keep them under control by snipping bits off to use in hearty soups and winter stews. These "prunings" will also release their scent to remind you of hot summer days. From left to right, starting at top left: basil, chives, mint, oregano, parsley, rosemary, sage, thyme.

When you move your mint outdoors in the spring, plunge the pot into the ground to keep its rampant root growth under control.

Chives (*Allium*)

Freeze-dried chives are no match for the mild oniony flavour of just-snipped chives. Try garlic chives (*A. tuberosum*) for a mild garlic taste. Plant it in rich, moist soil and keep it well watered. Chives don't mind warmer temperatures, unlike most other herbs. Trim the plant to keep its growth continual and to prevent it from becoming unkempt. Cats are partial to chives, so you might give the extra bits to your pet.

Mint (*Mentha*)

Mint has the ability to grow taller than most of the herbs I've described here. Pinch or prune to keep its growth easy to manage. Try many of the varieties now available — spearmint, peppermint, and golden apple are just three. Mint grows best in rich, moist soil, can tolerate some shade, and likes cool temperatures.

Oregano (*Origanum*)

The most flavourful oregano is called Greek oregano — use it in any tomato dish for a great taste. Seeds can be slow to germinate and can produce plants that lack flavour, so buy a healthy plant from a garden centre or herb farm or start a cutting from a friend's bush. It needs a lot of light and will do best in a light well-drained soil. In fact, the dry atmosphere of many Canadian homes in the winter is well suited to oregano's needs. Keep the plant bushy by cutting back frequently before it flowers (toss the clippings into sauces, soups, and stews).

Parsley (*Petroselinum*)

For a selection of parsley, grow a pot of curly parsley and one of Italian, which has flatter leaves. Both prefer a cool situation and frequent watering. They can also tolerate some shade. When growth slows, replace with a new plant.

Rosemary (*Rosmarinus officinalis*)

Rosemary can be grown into a small bush as a houseplant, but it likes a cool location. Its grey-green, stiff leaves give off a sweet scent. It's a slow grower and will drop its leaves if the temperature is too warm, if the soil is too dry (like most perennial herbs brought indoors, rosemary needs frequent watering), or if its soil is not alkaline enough. A small dose of lime or wood ashes added to the surface of the soil will keep it alkaline. Fluorescent lights are a must for rosemary's success.

Sage (*Salvia*)

Not everyone succeeds in growing sage indoors, but it's worth a try. To increase your chance of success grow it under lights, or it could lose its leaves. Ordinary potting soil will do as long as it drains well. Give it full sun and fertilize if you take frequent cuttings.

Thyme (*Thymus*)

Thyme is a low-growing plant that forms a mat of tiny greyish leaves. Cutting back the tips will keep it bushy and provide seasoning for soups, salad dressings, omelettes, for example. It likes well-drained soil.

Transplant seedlings into individual pots when several pairs of leaves have formed. Carefully nudge the plant from the growing medium, holding only the first leaves.

Make a small hole in the new soil to receive the seedling.

Insert the seedling, aligning the top of the soil with the level of the first leaves. Firm the soil around the stem. Finish by watering gently.

1. Gather the sterile containers the seedlings will be transplanted into. You might be using another group of flats or paper or peat pots, or even such "found" containers as foam coffee cups, the bottom of cardboard milk cartons, or frozen-juice containers. The advantage of paper or peat pots is that eventually they can be transplanted directly into the ground, where the paper or peat will decompose, leaving the roots undisturbed.

2. Fill the containers with a moist, light commercial potting mixture. Use a pencil or dibble to make small indentations in the soil to receive the seedling. Most seedlings at this stage should be planted 2.5 to 5 cm (1 to 2 inches) apart.

3. Carefully hold the seedling by its seed leaf (the cotyledon), *not* the stem, roots, or delicate true leaves. Using tweezers or a blunt stick, gently tease the seedling out of the soil. If your seedlings are growing fairly close together, you may be able to get them out only in small bunches. If this is the case, carefully separate them once you have removed them from the container.

4. Insert the seedling in the new container, making sure the soil comes up to the level of the seed leaves. Pat the soil around the seedling and water gently.

5. Let the transplanted seedlings have a few days to recover from the shock. Don't immediately put them under strong lighting, but gradually expose them to brighter light by moving them closer to the window or lowering the fluorescent lights. If they start to get leggy or spindly, give them more light.

6. Start to fertilize the seedlings on a weekly basis with a diluted water-soluble fertilizer, such as 20-20-20, until they are ready for hardening off, which will be discussed in Chapter 3.

Rule of Thumb

High temperature and low light will result in spindly seedlings that will struggle to live when transplanted.

Thin out seedlings that are weak. They will never be as productive as the stronger seedlings. Throw them in the compost.

The Cold Frame in February

Snow that gathers on the cold frame can be left there as extra insulation for the crops and plants inside the frame. Leaving the snow on for a couple of weeks in the colder regions won't harm the crops because they're not growing at this time of year.

In milder regions, if you're growing some of the hardier green crops such as corn salad, keep any accumulations of snow off the cover of the frame to allow sunlight into the frame.

Kids' Gardening:
Making a Cactus Dish Garden

There's something about cacti that attracts children — maybe it's their weird and wonderful shapes, maybe it's their easy care. Whatever it is, putting together a cactus dish garden is a good way to introduce children to the care of plants. And taking a child to buy the cactus plants can be an entertaining outing for child and grown-up alike.

While you're shopping, pick up a bag of special soil for growing cacti in and some gravel for drainage. If you haven't a suitable dish at home, get one at the garden centre at the same time. The dish should be made of plastic, ceramic, or glass, with a depth of about 13 cm (5 inches) and a minimum diameter of 18 cm (7 inches). Four plants will be enough for a dish of this size. A pair of leather gloves to wear when handling the cacti are needed, too (although you can use tongs to pick them up).

Here are some cactus plants that you might look out for. I've chosen ones that are specially recommended for window-sill growing; the main requirement is a sunny window.

Old man cactus (*Cephalocereus senilis*), with its woolly "hair," is a cactus children are drawn to. It's very slow growing and will never reach its mature height of 60 cm (10 feet) in a dish garden! It is grey-green and has soft hairy spines.

Pincushion cactus (*Mammillaria*) has a round shape with spines. Depending on the variety, it can have silky hair.

Prickly pear (*Opuntia microdasys*) is one of the most familiar cacti, and is easy to care for. Its flat round or oval pads grow from a thick central pad and it has barbed bristles.

Urchin cactus (*Echinopsis*) is a rounded cactus with distinctive ribs on which prickly spines grow.

Putting the garden together is simplicity itself. Place a 5 cm (2-inch) layer of gravel on the bottom of the container and cover with about an inch of soil (to within 5 cm/2 inches of the top). Before adding the plants, move them around on the table while they're still in their pots to get the most pleasing arrangement. Then carefully remove the plants, either wearing the gloves or using the tongs, and place them in the container. Fill with 2.5 cm (1 inch) of soil. If you like, you can add a thin layer of small gravel. Let the plants settle for a day or two, then water with a fine mist. Cacti never need much water, but will require more in the spring and summer, when they are usually growing, than in the other seasons. Allow soil to dry completely between waterings — as with most other houseplants, they will suffer from too much water rather than too little.

Let your child's imagination expand the theme — adding a plastic skull to the desert scene brings fun into gardening.

A cactus dish garden can be as simple as a single cactus plant in a decorative, amusing pot.

February Gardening Checklist

❧ Bring in more branches from spring-flowering trees and shrubs such as magnolia and cherry.

Ornamental Garden

❧ Take geraniums out of storage, repot, water well, and put in well-lit spot.
❧ Repot and prune indoor plants.

Zones 2 to 6

❧ Repair storm damage to trees and shrubs.
❧ Sow seeds for perennial flowers.

Zones 7 to 9

❧ Remove debris from flower beds.
❧ Lift and divide perennials.
❧ Remove thatch on lawn and aerate (see Chapter 4).
❧ Prune ornamental trees and summer-flowering shrubs (see Chapter 4).
❧ Deadhead early bulbs when blooming is complete. Leave foliage. Divide snowdrops after flowering.
❧ Sow sweet peas outdoors.
❧ Sow hardy annual seeds indoors.
❧ Plant lily bulbs.
❧ Plant trees and shrubs, weather permitting.
❧ Plant bare-root roses if unable to do so in January.

Fruit and Vegetable Garden

Zones 2 to 6

❧ Toward the end of the month or early March, start seeds indoors for vegetables such as cabbage, onions, leeks, and leafy greens, herbs such as chives and parsley, and more perennials.

Zones 7 to 9

❧ Prune fruit trees (see Chapter 7).
❧ Prune bush and cane fruits and plant new ones.
❧ Sow parsley outdoors.
❧ Start seed for annual herbs.
❧ Work compost or manure into vegetable bed.
❧ Sow salad crops in cold frame in midmonth. Sow broad beans, leeks, radishes, and shallots in cold frame at midmonth or outdoors at end of month.

Chapter 3

March

Great Expectations

March is a month of great expectations and sometimes dashed hopes as Mother Nature throws one last snowstorm at us. The sun feels warmer, but wind still carries winter's chill. In milder zones, such as those on the West Coast, spring is well under way. Gardeners there have already been through the on-again, off-again nature of spring.

No matter where you garden, though, this is the time of year when you're ready to get out and get digging — but before you do, you should know something about the soil you're so eager to plunge your shovel into. An understanding of soil, and your soil in particular, will help you get the most of out of it and grow more productive plants.

The soil feeds your plants. It stores and releases to plants the nutrients they need to grow; acts as an anchor for the plant, to prevent it from being swept away by wind or water; and provides a home to the micro-organisms that decompose organic materials and help plant growth. As well, knowing about your soil can help you decide how to *improve* it, which is one of the most important things you can do to extend the growing season and add to the health of your garden.

Soil

Soil is composed of rock and mineral particles of various sizes; humus — dead and decaying organic material; water; air; and living creatures, including everything from earthworms to micro-organisms. Soils are categorized into sand, which has the largest particles; silt, which has small fine particles; and clay, which has very fine particles. When all three soil types are mixed with humus (or decomposed organic matter), the result is an excellent soil known as loam. Subcategories of soil composition are silty clay, silty clay loam, silty loam, loam, loamy sand, sandy loam, sandy clay loam, sandy clay, and clay loam.

As you can see, most soils are some combination of the three main soil textures, and that combination will affect the rate at which water passes through your soil, how long it is held there, the amount of air in the soil, how easy it is to work the soil, and how easily the soil will give up the nutrients to the plants.

🌱 Silt particles are larger than clay particles and smaller than sand particles. Silt holds its shape when you squeeze it. Silty soil can compact like clay, causing poor drainage.

Rule of Thumb

Don't work soil that is wet. Moist soil is manageable, but put off digging in soil that is drenched. You will cause it to compact, making it difficult for air to travel through it.

Advantages of chemical fertilizers

- Quickly released into the soil for use by the plant.
- Easy to control quantities used.
- Can be used for feeding of specific crops.
- Disease-free.

Disadvantages of chemical fertilizers

- Provide no organic matter.
- Can kill earthworms.
- Can actually cause plants to become weakened when used improperly.
- Care must be taken in their use to avoid overdoses.
- Don't always contain trace elements.
- Can become expensive.
- Can tempt you into looking for the "quick fix," instead of concentrating on soil improvement.
- Require a great deal of energy to manufacture.

Rule of Thumb

If you use chemical fertilizers, you still need to add humus (in the form of compost, for example) to the soil.

Sources of nutrients and organic fertilizers

Nitrogen: Bloodmeal, bone meal, fish meal, Canola-seed meal, manure.

Phosphorus: Bone meal, rock phosphate.

Potassium: Manure, wood ashes, liquid seaweed, kelp meal, green sand.

Renewing Soil in the Vegetable Garden

If your vegetable garden soil has not had compost added over the years, it is probably quite depleted and could do with a new lease on life. In most parts of the country, March might be a bit early to start digging the soil, but as soon as the frost is out of the ground and the soil isn't soaking wet (which could be in April or even May in some areas), start turning over the soil. If your soil is quite compacted, you should double-dig — that is, remove the top 30 cm (1 foot) or so and loosen the next 30 cm (1 foot) with a fork. Return the removed soil, adding and digging in manure, compost, and other organic material. If you've had your soil tested, add nutrients as identified by the test. If your soil is quite light, the double digging won't be necessary, but add as much organic material as you can find.

On a crisp March day, I find it very satisfying to dig a steaming pile of manure into my garden — a feeling maybe only gardeners and farmers can understand.

A more radical alternative is to take the vegetable bed out of production for the year and build it up by planting a succession of green-manure, or cover, crops that are dug in, then replaced by another crop. (See Chapter 10 for more information on cover crops.)

Rule of Thumb

When adding peat moss to your soil, make sure it is well dampened before you dig it in. Otherwise it will not absorb moisture once it's worked into the soil — the opposite of what you want.

The best time to add fertilizer is when preparing a new bed or planting. Digging in lots of compost or well-rotted manure might be all you have to do. However, you may know that your soil or the material you will be planting needs a boost. In these circumstances, it's best to use a dry or granular fertilizer because it can be dug in and released slowly. If you're applying dry fertilizer to established beds, scratch the fertilizer into the top of the soil around the plant. Don't let it come in contact with the plant or it will burn the parts it touches. Some liquid fertilizers can be applied directly to the foliage of the plant. With all fertilizers, read the directions carefully and then follow them exactly.

Different plants have different fertilizing needs, but generally it's unwise to apply fertilizer in the autumn because the plant will produce new tender growth that will be damaged in the cold weather. An exception is the application of fertilizers designated as slow release, which are usually applied in the late autumn. For example, lawns usually are given late-fall applications of slow-release fertilizers.

Raised Beds

Consider adding raised beds to your garden if you want to grow plants that have special soil requirements; if you want to do some intensive vegetable gardening; if you want your soil to warm up quickly in the spring and hold the warmth in the fall, thus extending your growing season. If you have heavy clay soil, you'll probably find it easier to install raised beds, rather than attempting to dig the clay.

I find an added bonus of my raised bed is that it provides a comfortable ledge to sit on, making weeding a little less tiresome.

Gardeners in most areas of the country can start to construct raised beds in March, but gardeners in colder regions may have to wait until later in the spring to begin construction. Raised beds have advantages for all gardeners, but northern gardeners can benefit especially. This type of bed offers the following advantages:

- Water will drain well.
- Walking around the beds will not compact the soil, causing distress to the roots.
- Cool air sinks, so your beds will be warmer earlier than those on ground level; therefore, you can plant them earlier.
- They are easy to tend if you have back or mobility problems.
- You can make the soil mix rich for intensive vegetable plantings.
- Plants' roots will grow deeply into the soil. Carrots, especially, do well in the fluffy, crumbly soil you can create in a raised bed.
- If you have solid clay soil, raised beds save you the backbreaking job of digging out the clay and replacing it with sandy loam. Just fill the new beds with the sandy loam over the clay.

When aren't raised beds advisable? If you're in a very dry or windy climate, the beds will dry out too quickly. You should also make sure that your raised beds won't create drainage problems for your neighbours.

Raised beds can be contained by railroad ties or wooden slats or beams (avoid creosoted wood of any kind, since its toxic chemicals will leach into the soil), rocks, brick, or cement. But if you prefer, you don't have to contain them at all. Just mound the earth up in the bed to the desired height. To prevent erosion, your soil should

be porous and rich in organic matter. Plantings around the edges with decorative herbs such as parsley and chives or flowers such as nasturtiums or marigolds will also help prevent soil erosion on these mounded beds. Make sure that the beds are not so long or wide that you can't easily reach all parts of them from the path. A width of about 1.2 m (4 feet) is comfortable for most people. A height of 20 to 30 cm (8 to 12 inches) is adequate.

Raised beds have many advantages — they drain well, they warm up quickly, and you can provide plants with their special soil needs.

You can dig over the area for a raised bed when the soil is warm enough, or prepare it in the fall for building the beds next spring. However, you can save yourself some work by just building and filling the raised bed with new soil without cultivating the soil underneath. The sod over which the raised bed is built will decompose in about six weeks as it is cut off from sunlight and as earthworms make their way to your fabulous new attraction. If this is the method you choose, though, avoid crops in the first year with long roots, such as carrots or parsnips.

Most urban gardeners won't have access to a free source of soil for the raised bed. Contact a local garden centre to see if they carry triple mix, a mixture that usually consists of one-third loam, one-third manure, and one-third topsoil. It's a one-time expense that will give your plants a good start. Build on this healthy start by adding compost and rotted manure in subsequent years.

Let the soil settle for several days to allow air pockets to fill. Add soil to maintain an even surface as settling occurs.

Use raised beds to get double duty from the cold frame. Build one of your raised beds to the same dimensions as a portable cold frame. You can then extend your gardening season even longer by setting the cold frame on the raised bed to add warmth.

If you are planning a series of raised beds, especially for vegetable growing, think carefully about the space you will need for paths. Like most of us, you'll want to make the best use of the — usually — limited space available to you. But don't make your paths too narrow. You might want to get a wheelbarrow between your beds, and when your plants are producing beyond your wildest dreams, they'll probably be spilling over into the paths to a certain extent. As you design and plant these beds, picture them filled with lush tomatoes, beans, peas, lettuce, squash, onions, carrots, for example. Then make your paths just a bit wider than you'd planned!

Once your beds are built and operating, it is advisable not to dig them too frequently. Some studies have shown that when you disturb the natural soil structure by turning it, you are actually causing it to compact. As long as you keep adding humus every year to the top of soil, the creatures in your soil — the micro-organisms and earthworms — will keep the soil sufficiently aerated.

Raised herb bed: You may be reluctant to go to the trouble of building raised beds and hauling in the large amounts of soil they need, but even so, you can start small by building a raised herb garden as a way of introducing yourself to gardening in raised beds. Herbs like sandy and warm soil. If your garden hasn't got these conditions, install a south-facing raised bed and fill it with a mixture of one part sand, two parts topsoil, and one part compost. You can make an attractive bed by building the walls of stone, which will also help warm the soil and hold the heat. Delicious and fragrant Mediterranean herbs such as rosemary and thyme will feel right at home in a bed such as this.

Starting a Compost Pile

If you haven't yet been a gardener who composts, this is the time to start. You've probably got a pretty good idea that I think organic material is vital for the success of your garden, whether your soil is sticky clay, sifting sand, or perfect loam. The best way to get organic material into your garden is by composting vegetable matter, kitchen scraps, and garden wastes to produce humus. You'll be helping not only your garden but also the garbage and landfill problem.

Composting is similar to what happens on the forest floor I mentioned earlier. Micro-organisms and earthworms decompose, or break down, organic material; the result is a crumbly dark mixture full of good things for your garden. But because you're taking a natural process and speeding it up, you have to be aware of the other elements of composting that you're trying to control: air and moisture. When these elements are in proper balance, you'll be able to produce compost on a constant basis and more quickly than it occurs in nature.

You can buy a bin for composting, or construct one yourself. In fact, a bin isn't strictly necessary, but in urban gardens, a bin can be set tidily out of the way.

Put your bin in a sunny spot if possible — the heat from the sun will help the micro-organisms do their work. Then all you have to do is start adding your wastes — fruit and vegetable scraps, disease-free garden prunings, lawn clippings. Try to keep the ingredients mixed up; for example, if you're adding several inches of grass clippings or leaves, layer them with some soil from your garden, other vegetable matter — even lint from your dryer!

Material that's been chopped up will decompose more quickly than larger pieces, so if you have a lot of broccoli stalks or cauliflower leaves, for instance, just chop them into pieces about the size of a walnut.

Oxygen is very important to the composting process. About once a week or so, give your compost pile a stir or turn it over now and then to be sure sufficient oxygen is available.

Another part of the decomposing process is water. If your bin is covered, thus preventing rain from providing moisture, add a bit of water every so often. The materials in your compost should be as moist as a squeezed sponge, not dripping, but not dry, either.

Reap the rewards of composting — dig in this homemade chock-full-of-nutrients plant food or use it as a mulch.

Once your bin is working, or "cooking," you will start to get finished compost — humus — in about three months. Depending on the style of bin you have, you might continually remove the compost from the bottom of the bin, or you might leave it alone until the bin is full and then start another pile beside it.

What you can compost: Compost anything that was once alive, except meat and animal products. Here are some suggestions:

coffee grounds

corncobs and stalks, chopped into
   2.5 cm (1-inch) pieces

eggshells

fruit peels

grass clippings

hair (avoid hair that's been dyed
   or permed)

hay

leaves

manure (not house-pet wastes)

peanut shells

pine needles

sawdust

seaweed

stable bedding

vegetable wastes

weeds (before seeds have set)

wood ash

wood chips

What you shouldn't compost: Although many of the following will break down, they shouldn't be composted because they attract rodents, harbour or cause disease, or contain toxins:

bones

cat litter or any pet excrement

coal ashes

dairy products

diseased plants

fatty or oily foods

fish and meat

Browns and greens

Variety is the spice of life, but variety is even more important in the compost pile — it's what makes the best compost. Looking at the list of materials that can be composted, you'd think it wouldn't be hard to get that variety, and it isn't, but you have to be aware of a relationship that exists between different types of compostable materials. They're all organic, which means that they all contain carbon and nitrogen in varying degrees. The ratio of carbon content to the nitrogen content (C:N ratio) in the materials affects the speed with which they will break down. For speedy composting, the best ratio is between 20:1 and 30:1. How can you know the C:N ratio of every item that goes into the compost? You can't.

Instead, learn to think of materials as brown or green. Brown materials are high in carbon and green materials are high in nitrogen. By roughly balancing the browns and greens according to weight, you should have a fairly balanced mixture in the compost pile. Here are a few tips about browns and greens.

❧ Fresh grass clippings and fresh leaves are greens; dried grass clippings and dead leaves are browns.

❧ Browns usually have a high fibre content; greens have a low fibre content.

❧ Most materials of animal origin are high in nitrogen; this would include materials such as feathers, hair, and bloodmeal. Most dried materials of vegetable origin are high in carbon; this would include cornstalks, wood chips, and sawdust.

Ageratum

Growing Annuals from Seed

Growing annuals in the flower border helps to provide colour from spring to fall, bridging the gaps between perennials. Many people buy their annuals as seedlings in flats; others sow the seed outdoors in April or May. But by growing your annuals from seed, you get a headstart, save some money, and have some annuals you won't find in garden centres — and you'll also get a lot of pleasure from it.

Here are a few easy-to-grow-from-seed annuals that can be started indoors. Whether you start them in March or later in the spring depends on where you live and the type of seed; check the back of the seed package for specific information. And refer to the discussion in Chapter 2 on starting seeds for information about containers and growing medium, among other things.

Ageratum (*Ageratum*)

Their purple-blue, sometimes pink or white, fluffy flowers make a nice addition to the front or middle of a border; their height varies according to the variety — from 15 to 60 cm (6 inches to 2 feet). They like a bit of shade. Sow seeds six weeks before last frost date; in good light, they should germinate in five to fourteen days. Set seedlings out in full sun or partial shade after the last frost, 15 to 30 cm (6 to 12 inches) apart.

Black-eyed Susan Vine (*Thunbergia*)

Put black-eyed Susan vine in a hanging basket, or give it a trellis to twine around and show off its yellow, orange, or cream-coloured flowers. Start seeds indoors about eight weeks before the last frost. Keep in a warm spot. Germination is slow. Transplant to containers or ground after last frost, providing support for its vigorous growth.

Burning Bush (*Kochia*)

Although burning bush does produce flowers, they are quite inconspicuous. The plant makes a good temporary hedge 60 to 90 cm (2 or 3 feet) tall. Its slender, pale-green leaves can also add interest to the midborder; as nights grow cooler, the foliage turns purple-red. Two or three weeks before the last frost, sow seeds indoors; put the pots under plastic in a warm place. Germination is fast — within days. Transplant outdoors when danger of frost is past. The plant self-sows and can become a pest.

Butterfly Flower (*Schizanthus*)

Also known as poor man's orchid, the white, pink, or lavender flowers do resemble those of an orchid. It grows to 60 cm (2 feet) and makes good cut flowers. Sow the seeds indoors eight weeks before the last frost; they need dark to germinate. Germination times can vary from several days to several weeks, so don't give up on it. Transplant to a partially shady spot in rich, well-drained soil.

China Aster (*Callistephus chinensis*)

This annual's colours cover a wide spectrum: white, pink, red, violet-blue, and purple. It has a long blooming season and makes a good cut flower. The seeds need an early start — as early in March as possible, or even in February. It will grow to 30 to 75 cm (1 to 2½ feet); the flowers are similar to those of chrysanthemums. Sow the seeds 3 mm (⅛ inch) deep and keep at room temperature; germination will take place in a couple of weeks. Transplant outdoors to a sunny or partially shady spot after danger of frost has passed.

Cosmos (*Cosmos*)

Cosmos will self-seed readily, but if you want to try some new varieties, it's easy to start from seed. A virtual rainbow of colours is available: pale yellow, orange, red, pink, magenta, purple, and white. With its height (some grow as tall as 1.2 m/4 feet) and its ferny foliage, it looks lovely at the back of the border. Sow seeds six weeks before last frost and cover lightly with growing medium. Set transplants 20 to 30 cm (8 to 12 inches) apart in early summer.

Cupflower (*Nierembergia*)

Blue, lavender, or white cup-shaped flowers grow on this short (15 cm/6-inch) plant. It forms dense mats and is good for window boxes, containers, rock gardens, or between paving stones. Sow indoors twelve weeks before the last frost; germination is slow — about a month. After the last frost, transplant seedlings to a spot with full sun and well-drained soil. Keep well watered. Some shade is advisable where summers are very hot.

Cosmos

Gazania *(Gazania)*

The daisylike flowers bloom in cream, yellow, golden-orange, bronze, pink, or red. Gazania grows to about 38 cm (15 inches) and forms sturdy clumps about 36 cm (14 inches) wide. It stands up well to drought and heat, but also tolerates a light frost. About eight weeks before the last frost, sow the seeds 3 mm (1/8 inch) deep and put in a warm spot. They will germinate in about a week. Transplant outdoors after the last frost to a sunny spot in well-drained soil.

Heliotrope *(Heliotropium)*

The sweet-scented heliotrope (also known as cherry pie) has flowers of lavender, purple, or white, and dark-green leaves. It will grow to 60 cm (2 feet). Sow seeds indoors in a warm spot about three months before last frost; germination is slow (up to six weeks). Don't rush to transplant outdoors — be sure all danger of frost has passed. It does best in a sunny spot and should be kept well watered. Expect blooms about four months after germination.

Lisianthus *(Eustoma)*

Evidently this is known as "Canada pest" in the southern plain states of the United States, where it's considered a weed. It's certainly an attractive weed, with bell-shaped flowers of blue, cream, pink, lilac, or deep blue. The foliage is grey-green. They grow to about 60 cm (2 feet), and make good cut flowers. Sow seeds in very early March (though some gardeners do so as early as December). Keep them in a warm place and they will germinate in two or three weeks. After five weeks, transplant to pots of rich soil and keep in a sunny spot. Don't overwater. Transplant to a sunny or partially shaded spot in the garden after the last frost.

Heavenly blue morning glory, doing a good job of hiding its support.

ABOVE RIGHT:
Verbena's clusters of small flowers show off well when planted in clumps and are equally attractive in planters with other flowers.

Lobelia *(Lobelia)*

Nothing can match lobelia cascading out of a hanging basket or window box. Its small and copious blue, purple, or white flowers show off many other flowers to advantage. Sow the seed about eight weeks before the last frost. Keep out of direct sun, under a clear cover, in a cool spot, especially after germination, which takes two or three weeks. They can be transplanted outside after the last frost date, in partial or full shade. They'll bloom about eight weeks after germination, but flowering will slow down or stop in very hot weather. Cut them back if this happens, and they will start blooming again when the weather cools.

Morning Glory *(Ipomoea)*

Find something for a morning glory to scramble up and you'll never tire of its white, pink, purple, or blue flowers. It can grow to 3 m (10 feet) in a single season. The seeds need to be soaked overnight or filed lightly to break their coats before sowing. About a month before the last frost, plant them 1.25 cm ($^1/_2$ inch) deep in peat pots and put in a warm spot. Germination should occur in about a week. Transplant after the last frost, in a sunny spot.

Painted Tongue *(Salpiglossis)*

The trumpet-shaped flowers bloom in a wide range of colours: apricot, yellow, bronze, shades of brown, dark red, and various hues of blue and purple. The plant can reach

1 m (3 feet). Six weeks before the last frost, start indoors. The seeds need dark to germinate, which they will do in about three weeks. Transplant when danger of frost has passed, in full sun or partial shade.

Verbena *(Verbena)*

Verbena makes a nice addition to the flower bed or container planting with its rich reds, purples, and blues; there are white varieties, as well. They grow from 15 to 25 cm (6 to 10 inches) in height. Sow seeds indoors about eight weeks before last frost; they need dark to germinate, which happens in about two weeks. Transplant after danger of frost has passed, in a sunny spot with rich soil.

The Cold Frame in March

Depending on your zone and last frost date, you can sow seeds directly into the cold frame in March for planting out in the garden at a later date.

Some vegetables that take well to this treatment are lettuce, cabbage, broccoli, Swiss chard, kale. Sow the seeds as you would in a flat, remembering to mark the rows. Cover lightly with soil and mist gently with water. They won't dry out as quickly as seedlings grown in the house, since their roots can burrow into the earth for moisture.

A well-equipped cold frame has a thermometer and an automatic vent opener.

Controlling heat in the cold frame: Heat can build up surprisingly quickly in a cold frame in the spring and fall months, even on cloudy days. Whatever the season, it is a good idea to keep a thermometer in the cold frame; a thermometer that records maximum and minimum temperatures will let you keep track of the range of temperatures in your frame. Protect the thermometer from the direct rays of the sun so that it is measuring the temperature of the air inside the frame, not the heat of the direct rays.

The temperature in the cold frame should not be allowed to go higher than 30°C (85°F). Control the temperature by opening and closing the cover of the frame. If you're a gardener who isn't at home for most of the day, you can install an automatic vent. This gadget is a piston that is activated by heat; as the temperature rises, the piston will force the cover open; as the temperature falls, the piston allows the cover to close.

If you're at home during the day, use a simple notched stick to keep the cover open.

The Hot Frame

Hot frames are not new ideas. In our grandparents' day, fresh manure was used to heat the frame. A pit dug to about 60 cm (2 feet) was filled with the fresh manure and straw. Then a layer of straw and topsoil was added. This method was used to get an early start in spring.

A cold frame can also be turned into a hot frame by using soil-warming or air-warming cables. Naturally, you won't be able to move the hot frame around as easily, but you can extend your growing season even more by using cables.

Experiment with the hot frame—other than in the Far North, you might have success in using it for germination.

Kids' Gardening: Composting with Worms

While *you* may have qualms about composting indoors with worms, chances are your kids will love the idea.

The size of the container will depend on how much food waste you expect to feed the worms every day, but a good size is 60 by 90 cm (2 by 3 feet) and 30 cm (1 foot) deep. This will take about 450 g (1 pound) of food scraps a day.

The box can be made of wood, metal, or plastic; you can also buy boxes specially built for worms. The important thing is that the bin have ventilation holes in the bottom. Indoors, a rubber mat placed under the bin will catch any liquid runoff; the bin should sit on blocks for good air circulation. The best place for the bin is a basement, because worms like cool temperatures.

The worm bin should have some kind of bedding material, such as shredded dampened newspaper (but not colour sections), straw, soil, or shredded dead leaves or leaf mould, or a combination. Layer the materials: 8 to 10 cm (3 or 4 inches) of the bedding material on the bottom, and over that 5 cm (2 inches) of soil. Dampen by spraying with water until the bedding material has the consistency of a wrung-out sponge.

You need special worms for your bin, not regular garden worms. They can be purchased from gardening centres or specialty suppliers; be sure to get redworms or African night crawlers and not dew worms. For the box I just described, purchase about 1 kg (2 pounds) of worms. This is a one-time expense, since the worms will reproduce. Add them to the box—they will quickly burrow into the bedding material. Cover the box and keep it covered. Chop up food waste into small pieces to add to the bin. (Don't add meat or dairy products.)

Over the next few months, the level of the bedding material will fall, since the worms will be consuming it as well as the food wastes. When you want to "harvest" some of the finished compost, take off the lid, and remove a layer of the compost. Return any worms to the bin; set recognizable pieces of food aside to be put back in the bin later. Keep scooping out layers in this fashion.

When you've reached the bottom, dump the worms into another container while you add new bedding material and start the cycle all over again.

The compost from worm bins is full of nutrients and can be added to potting soil or garden beds. Your child will probably want to use it for his or her garden patch.

*Worm composter courtesy of Original Vermicomposter, Vermitech Systems.

March Gardening Checklist

- ❧ Check garden tools and equipment; repair and sharpen as needed.
- ❧ Increase watering of houseplants and fertilize lightly.
- ❧ Start compost pile.

Ornamental Garden

- ❧ Prune ornamental trees and shrubs that bloom on new wood; cut honeysuckle back to one or two main stems; cut thyme and lavender back to ground level (see Chapter 4).
- ❧ Check for perennials whose roots have been shoved out of the ground by freeze-thaw-freeze cycles. Either gently push the roots back into the ground or cover with some compost.
- ❧ Start tuberous begonias in pots.
- ❧ Start seeds indoors for annual flowers.

Zones 2 to 6

- ❧ Lift and divide perennials.
- ❧ Remove leaves and winter debris from lawn. Dethatch and aerate if necessary.
- ❧ Prune ornamental trees and shrubs.
- ❧ Root hardwood cuttings.
- ❧ Plant evergreens and conifers.

Zones 7 to 9

- ❧ Remove winter mulches, weed flower beds and apply new mulch of compost.
- ❧ Fertilize lawns. Seed or sod new lawns.
- ❧ Prune, fertilize, and top-dress roses. Continue to plant new roses.
- ❧ Harden off annual seedlings.
- ❧ Plant perennials, and lift and divide any not yet moved.
- ❧ Plant summer bulbs (see Chapter 8).
- ❧ Plant evergreens.

Fruit and Vegetable Garden

Zones 2 to 6

- ❧ Prune fruit trees, blueberry bushes, bramble fruits, and grape vines (see Chapter 7).
- ❧ Set out cold frames and row covers.
- ❧ Continue sowing vegetable seeds indoors. Be guided by your last frost date and information on seed packets.

Zones 7 to 9

- ❧ Finish pruning fruit trees and bushes.
- ❧ Spread compost or well-rotted manure on vegetable bed.
- ❧ Start outdoor sowing of radish, garlic, broad beans (in first half of month); peas, beans, spinach, leaf lettuce, onions, and turnips (in second half of month).
- ❧ Sow heat-loving vegetables such as tomatoes indoors or in cold frame.
- ❧ Start to harden off and transplant cold-frame seedlings, beginning with lettuce.

Spring

In A BOOK ABOUT EXTENDING THE GARDENING SEASON to a complete, year-round activity in a country as vast and variable as Canada, you might wonder what could be said about spring. It is, after all, regardless of geographic region, the universally acknowledged beginning of our gardening year. Everything that needs doing in the garden *seems* to need doing in the spring.

Well, this section has great news for you. Spring is not the season you extend your physical limitations all the way to the chiropractor's. With some planning during the winter months, you will have done much of the "spade work" that will lead you gently into a beautiful spring season that is rich in its rewards.

Like an extra-early tomato crop.

Baskets full of living colour in May and June.

A landscape that is well established and substantially disease- and insect-free.

This is the stuff of the *new* spring.

The spring season I will introduce you to in this section helps you pace your garden's performance and maximize the potential of it through pruning techniques, soil prepreparation, early seed sowing, and—one of my favourite topics—mulching.

I love mulching because I would just as soon take the time to enjoy the full flowering potential of my garden as bend over for endless hours weeding it.

And, finally, I am reminded of the poor street person whose tin cup remained empty when he put out a sign that read "I am blind," but whose tin cup filled up after he changed his sign to read "It is spring and I am blind."

The sign I want to post at the beginning of this section is "It is spring and I wish to enjoy the benefits of a gorgeous yard year-round!"

Chapter 4

April

The Unpredictable Month

April is both an exciting and a tricky month. In most parts of the country, the early bulbs are up, and new growth in the ornamental garden appears almost overnight. At this time of year, though, frosts, even snowfalls, are still part of the weather mix.

You might be tempted to start removing some of the mulch you applied late the previous fall, but it's best to leave it in place for now. It's true that it will keep the soil cool even on warm sunny days, but it also does the more important job of protecting the plants from the freeze-thaw cycles that often occur in spring. (For more information on mulches, see Chapter 6, and for information on plant protection, see Chapter 5.)

Pruning Plants

Before the general gardening tasks divert your attention, this is a good time to undertake some maintenance in the form of pruning. Many people avoid pruning because it seems a scary undertaking. They're afraid of taking off too much, too little, too soon, too late, or the wrong branch. But once you understand a few basics, it's a job you'll approach with confidence. Although any heavy pruning, such as on large trees, should be done by an expert, you can carry out most jobs on your own.

Why is it necessary to prune? At this time of year, pruning to get rid of damaged limbs is an obvious reason, and a task that is easily accomplished; you can see what needs cutting and where. At other times of the year, you'll find yourself considering pruning to control disease; to encourage flowering and the production of fruit or foliage — in other words, for better yields; and to contain or direct growth in some fashion. However, not every plant needs to be pruned every year.

Controlling disease: Although you may want to control most diseases with commercial products made for a particular disease, there are two diseases best handled by pruning: black knot and fire blight. Black knot is a fungal disease that you're most likely to find on plum and cherry trees; you can identify it by the black galls (knotty growths) that appear on the bark of these trees. Fire blight is a bacterial disease that causes new shoots of infected shrubs to wilt, turn black, and die; you're likely to find it on roses and mountain ash. Make your pruning cut just beyond the diseased wood and destroy all the diseased branches; do not add to the compost pile. Keep your pruning implements clean by wiping them with rubbing alcohol or household bleach between cuts to avoid infecting good wood.

*Spring chores in the garden,
such as pruning (BELOW), aren't
difficult to do when flowers
like these cheerful tulips begin
to bloom, reminding us of the
colourful and plentiful blooms
ahead. Suntraps, like the wall
of the solarium, help provide
warmth for plants to bloom
earlier than in other spots.*

The attentive gardener promotes health in plants by pruning diseased parts, such as the galls on this forsythia.

Preventive medicine plays a role heading off any disease before it gets a foothold. This is accomplished by cutting out branches that are damaged — look for broken or split bark — or in poor health — look for galls, gummy twigs and bark, and sunken bark (indicates canker). Branches that cross, especially if they are rubbing together, should be pruned out, and not only for aesthetic reasons. Such branches can open a wound at the point of contact, providing an entryway for disease and weakening the system of the entire plants. Insects love weakened plants, so keep your plants healthy by checking for these crossed limbs and pruning them out.

Encouraging production: Every gardener wants a better yield and one that will continue for as long as possible. Whether you're pinching out the tips of growing tomatoes in order to produce more flowers or cutting a vine back to the ground to promote more vigorous growth, you're pruning to encourage production. Plants want to produce seed to continue their lineage, so to speak; as long as they're thwarted — by pruning — they will continue to attempt to produce seed, which is usually preceded by the production of flowers or fruit.

Can I ever overprune? is one of the most frequently asked gardening questions. The best answer is a definite "Not likely." In fact, the only serious damage that can occur from heavy pruning is when hardwood "bleeders" such as maples, birch, and mulberries are pruned in spring. Beyond these, there is little likelihood that pruning damage can occur. On the other hand, an unpruned hardy plant can become prone to disease and insects, a poor bloomer, and a downright eyesore. Left to their own devices, some woody ornamentals can grow so out of control that they're beyond repair.

An important pruning principle is to keep the centre of shrubs open so that light can penetrate and air can circulate freely. This not only cuts down on disease, but encourages the strong healthy limbs to produce better flowers and foliage.

Directing growth: Directing growth can cover everything from topiary to espaliering to pruning for attractiveness. Some plants are pruned to keep their rampant growth within limits; to improve their shape; to encourage growth in a new direction; to rejuvenate overgrown shrubs; and to remove suckers.

Pruning Tools

After using any cutting tool, clean the blades with steel wool, then oil lightly.

Hedge or grass shears: These can be used for light jobs such as pruning evergreens or trimming a hedge.

Pruning shears (secateurs): Use pruning shears for removing shoots and small stems. Pruning shears are available in two styles: the "duck-billed," which has two curved blades; and the anvil type, which has two straight blades. The duck-billed shears are easier to manoeuvre in small spaces and give a cleaner cut than the anvil type. I find duck-billed shears perfect for pruning out the inside branches of large shrubs like dogwood or viburnum. A safety lock is an important feature. Prolong the life of your pruning shears by not attempting to use them on branches that are too thick for the size of the blades.

Pruning knife: A sharp knife comes in handy for tidying up cuts. Look for one with a curved blade, as well as a curved handle for easy gripping.

Lopping pruners: Use long-handled lopping pruners for large stems. They come in a variety of weights, the lightest meant for cutting small branches and the heaviest for large branches.

Pruning saw: Use a pruning saw for cutting large branches and dead wood. There are many styles with straight or curved blades that taper at the end. Folding pruning knives are also a constant companion year-round—useful for everything from cutting twine to slicing an apple for inspection.

Chain saw: Most urban gardeners can get along without a chain saw. For large properties with big pruning jobs, however, it's a good tool to have.

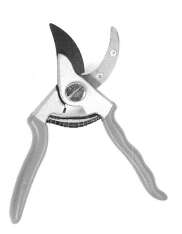

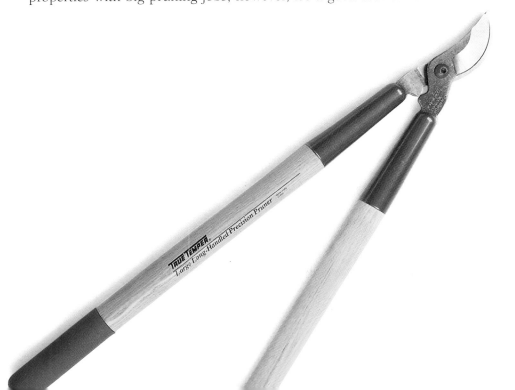

> ### Rule of Thumb
> If you have a big pruning job ahead of you — for example, when a vine such as bittersweet or honeysuckle has grown out of control — spread the pruning over several years. Take out a third of the growth this year, then let the plant recover. Tackle another third next year, and finish up in the third year. The plant will not be overly stressed and the pruning will not be a blot on your garden picture.

It's not necessary to have a large arsenal of pruning implements, but secateurs and loppers are two basics that should look after most jobs.

Rule of Thumb

To improve the flowering of wisteria, cut back the new shoots in the summer.

When to Prune

I remember a friend telling me how he had chopped a couple of feet off a large forsythia bush in March — only to watch the branches flower in their neatly tied bundles at the curb! Thus, one of the most important considerations in pruning flowering and fruiting trees and shrubs is knowing when to prune. You need to leave enough time for the plant to recover from the pruning if it's going into a stressful season such as winter and to produce new growth. In order to choose the right time and prune successfully, you'll have to be familiar with your plant's habits. The two most important things to know are when it flowers and whether it flowers on old or new growth.

Prune spring-flowering shrubs immediately after they have flowered. These plants start to form next year's buds very soon after their blossoms fade. Prune summer-flowering shrubs in the fall or winter, for they will make flower buds on the current year's growth — that is, the growth that is put forth in the spring bears the flowers that will bloom later in the summer.

Spring-flowering shrubs and vines that flower on last year's wood: Prune these immediately after they bloom, cutting them back by at least one-third. Remove the wood that has carried the blossoms and keep the new strong shoots.

> Bigleaf hydrangea (*Hydrangea macrophyla*)
> *Buddleia alternifolia*
> *Clematis armandii*
> Deutzia (*Deutzia*)
> Flowering currant (*Ribes sanguineum*)
> Forsythia (*Forsythia*)
> Honeysuckle (*Lonicera*)
> Mock orange (*Philadelphus*)
> *Spiraea arguta*
> Wisteria (*Wisteria*)

Summer-flowering shrubs and vines that flower on new shoots: Prune back last year's shoots to two or three buds or shoots in late winter or spring just as growth begins. It might seem drastic, but these shrubs will reward you with large blooms. Cut the older wood only if you want to change the shrub's shape. It's a good idea to mulch the plant after pruning and to fertilize moderately.

> Bluebeard (*Caryopteris*)
> Butterfly bush (*Buddleia davidii*)
> *Clematis jackmanii*
> False spirea (*Sorbaria*)
> Hills of snow hydrangea (*Hydrangea arborescens grandiflora*)
> Peegee hydrangea (*Hydrangea paniculata grandiflora*)
> Redroot *Ceanothus* (deciduous types)
> Spanish broom (*Genista hispanica*)
> *Spiraea bumalda*
> *Spiraea japonica*
> Sumac (*Rhus*)

Pruning Tips for Trees

If you're taking those first nervous steps with loppers in hand, here are some conditions that are improved by pruning. Just concentrating on these will give you confidence.

Pruning out a competing leader: Occasionally the leading shoot of a tree will produce a strong secondary shoot that competes with the leading shoot, giving the tree an unbalanced look. Remove such a shoot where it branches off from the leading shoot. Make the cut on the diagonal, just above an outward-facing bud, to encourage the competitor to bush out from the cut. This type of pruning should be done when the tree is not actively growing.

Removing water spouts: Water spouts are those slender shoots that grow on the trunk of a tree. They may appear where a branch has been removed. On mature trees, cut them off flush with the trunk. On young trees, remove them when the trunk of the tree is the height you want.

One of the most obvious examples of this in my garden is the honey locust tree. I simply snap off the young feathery growth with my fingers every spring.

Removing larger branches: It's sometimes necessary to remove a larger branch for aesthetic reasons — it may have grown too large compared with the other branches, resulting in a lopsided or awkward growth, or it's growing back into the centre of the tree. Cut such branches to about one-third, at a point where a side shoot is growing in the same direction.

If the branch is fairly substantial, reduce its length to about 46 cm (18 inches). You might do this in several stages so that you're always dealing with lighter, more manageable amounts of discarded limb. To avoid stripping bark down the trunk of the tree, cut the remaining stump from the bottom, about one-third of the way through, then make the final cut from the top, flush with the main trunk.

For more about pruning fruit trees and fruiting shrubs, see Chapter 7.

Rule of Thumb

The best time to prune trees other than bleeders is when they are dormant. Bleeders are trees whose sap runs after they've been cut.

One of the easiest jobs is removing water spouts, especially if you prune them when they're still young.

Use a pruning saw for larger jobs, such as getting rid of this obtrusive branch.

Pruning Shrubs and Vines

If a shrub is showing signs of age — few flowers, scraggly growth, many suckers — you can give it a new lease on life by judicious pruning. In the spring, cut the branches to various heights, removing one-third of the oldest, woodiest growth from the bottom of the shrub and maintaining an attractive shape. Take out the scraggly growth and suckers. Fertilize and mulch.

For general pruning of shrubs and vines, look for dead or damaged wood and cut it back to an outward-facing bud or shoot. Next, remove any weak shoots, cutting back to the main branch. Unattractive or straggly branches can be cut back by half, again at an angle, just above an outward-facing bud or shoot. Take care not to remove healthy branches that will flower later in the season.

Suckers: Suckers are new shoots that grow from the root or base of a plant. Not all suckers have to be removed, but if a plant is spreading beyond its bounds, you will need to get rid of the suckers. When a plant has been grafted on to a different root stock, the suckers can weaken the growth of the plant.

I remember visiting a garden once and being asked to identify a very straggly shrub. After half an hour of pruning, we uncovered a beautiful weeping caragana specimen that had been hidden by years of unchecked sucker growth from its understock.

If the sucker comes from the variety — that is, above the join with the root stock — it can be left to grow. Suckers can be pruned, but this will not prevent them from putting on new growth at the point of cutting. The best method is to follow the sucker back to the root, then pull it off by hand.

Pruning notes:

🌿 If you're shortening a branch, cut just above an outward-facing bud or shoot. Don't cut straight across but on the diagonal, in a line with the bud or shoot.

🌿 If you're removing a whole branch, cut it flush with the trunk or main branch. Always score through the bark on the underside of the limb to avoid stripping bark down the trunk.

Prune out unattractive stems on shrubs such as this wegelia.

Lilacs are notorious for sending out suckers, or shoots. Prune at soil level to keep their growth in check.

Pruning Roses for Better Blooming

If you like roses, you want them to bloom as prolifically and frequently as possible, and pruning is one way of ensuring larger, longer-lasting blooms. Pruning will also help the plants resist disease and insect attacks.

No matter where you live, you should prune your roses at the end of the dormant period and when all danger of frost has passed. In the milder parts of the country (zones 6 to 9), this could be January, but for most Canadians, April and May are the months. As with all gardening, there are a few exceptions, however. Ramblers and standard rose trees are pruned after flowering; climbing roses should be pruned lightly when they've finished flowering, as well as in the spring. Most roses flower on new growth (again, the exceptions are ramblers and most climbers).

Tools for pruning roses: Have at hand sharp pruning shears, long-handled loppers, and a narrow-bladed pruning saw. The shears are used for cutting shoots; the loppers are used for thicker stems; and the pruning saw is used on old wood that has become hard. I always wear my thickest pair of gardening gloves for this job, then shred and compost the cuttings in a separate pile. I use this compost as a mulch in an out-of-the-way corner of my garden.

Basic steps: Cut back all dead stems, then all thin or weak stems to where they meet a healthy stem. Finally, cut out stems that cross or rub, choosing the weaker of the two to discard.

Type of cut: If you're shortening a stem, find an outward-facing bud on the stem and make a cut not more than 6 mm (¹/₄ inch) above it. The cut should be angled at about forty-five degrees so that it slopes away from the bud and allows moisture to run off. If you're removing a whole stem, make your cut as close to the main stem as possible, using the hand pruners. Trim the stump with a sharp knife if necessary.

Find an outward-facing bud and cut just above it, at a forty-five-degree angle. This will encourage growth away from the centre of the bush and allow good air movement through the bush.

Pruning roses will ensure large blooms for a long period. Add a pair of thick gardening gloves to your equipment for rose pruning!

Rule of Thumb

When pruning roses, including deadheading, cut back to an outward-facing bud. This encourages an open bush through which air will circulate freely and sun will filter.

Prune hybrid tea roses when forsythia is in bloom.

Pruning new roses: Before planting a rose, check the roots and prune back any that are dead or damaged. Be careful not to overprune the roots, however, since the plant will need them to absorb moisture and nutrients. Cut off any dead wood.

Whether the rose is planted in the fall or spring, spring is the safest time to prune. Cut off all dead or damaged wood.

- Newly planted hybrid teas, grandifloras, and floribundas are pruned to about 13 cm (5 inches) from the ground.
- Newly planted species roses such as *Rosa rugosa* are pruned less severely because they bloom on the previous season's growth.
- Newly planted climbers, ramblers, and shrubs are pruned moderately.
- Newly planted polyanthas are cut back by one-third.
- Newly planted miniature roses are cut back to within 5 cm (2 inches) of the ground.

Pruning established roses: Follow the basic steps listed for all roses. Then proceed according to the type of rose you're pruning.

Hybrid teas, floribundas, and grandifloras: After first flowering, the top growth should be cut back by one-third. To get larger flowers, cut back harder, but this will also decrease the number of blooms. Grandifloras and floribundas don't need to be pruned as vigorously as hybrid teas to get the same result.

Species and shrub: Light pruning for shape is all that is necessary after the basic pruning steps have been followed. Cut back long shoots by one-third. Remove shoots that have no buds. Near the base of the shrub, cut any stems that have lost their vigour. Pruning the tips of stems will encourage stronger growth. Overgrown shrubs can be trimmed by removing one-third of the old wood.

Climbing roses: Lightly prune in summer after they have bloomed. Prune back to new buds. If you allow the seed pods (hips) to form, less energy will go into producing blooms and growth.

Ramblers: Prune after flowering. Remove the canes that bear the flowers that have just bloomed.

You can find roses in a wide variety of colours to complement other plantings.

Preparing a new rose bed in the spring

Later in the season, I keep the roses blooming by cutting off the spent flowers, a pruning practice known as deadheading.

Lawns

If you're eager to be out and about in the garden, there are some things you can do for your lawn at this time of year. With some fundamental preventive care now, you can cut down on the amount of time you'll have to spend on the lawn during the growing season. Don't work on the lawn if it's still wet, though, especially if your soil is clay.

Aerating: Having a large area of grass requires truly intensive gardening. A lawn is made up of hundreds of tiny grass plants, all with roots wanting to take in oxygen and nutrients. Over the years, the soil will become compacted, making it more difficult for air to enter. Every three or four years, either in the spring or fall, aerate the soil by using an aerator, which extracts plugs of soil. Sandy soil, of course, does not benefit from aerating, since it already drains well — too well, some might say!

You can rent machines for aerating or buy a simple hollow-pronged tool that will do the same thing. Leave the plugs where they fall and lightly top-dress the lawn with compost or good loam.

An avid gardener and golfer once told me that he always aerated his lawn by wearing a pair of golf shoes — the metal spikes did an excellent job.

A well-kept lawn shows off ornamental plants.

Dethatching: Thatch is a layer of grass roots (rhizomes) and leaf blades that weave themselves together around the individual grass plants that make up your lawn. Eventually the mat becomes so thick that air, water, and fertilizers have trouble getting down to the soil. Because the grass is not receiving the nutrients and moisture it needs, it becomes unhealthy and prone to insects and diseases.

Thatch buildup cannot entirely be prevented. However, you can retard the buildup if you encourage the grass roots to grow deeply into the soil: cut your grass to a height of 6 to 8 cm (2½ to 3 inches), water deeply, and aerate, as described earlier.

To see how thick the thatch layer in your lawn is, cut a core about 8 cm (3 inches) deep and examine it. If the thatch layer is less than 12 mm (½ inch), there's no cause for concern. If it's more than that, the thatch should be dealt with.

Use a rake or rent a dethatcher—a machine that cuts through the thatch and lifts it to the surface—if the thatch is particularly heavy. Rake up the thatch and add it to your compost. You can also use a commercial liquid dethatcher to do the job rather than the rake or rented dethatcher. (See Chapter 6 for more information about these dethatchers.)

Fertilizing: After a long, cold winter, lawns—like their owners—need a pick-me-up. The lawn's trip south comes in the handy shape of a bag. In the spring, lawns benefit from some added nitrogen as the grass goes into high-gear growth. A slow-release, granular 21-7-7 fertilizer is ideal, applied twice, six to eight weeks apart.

A dethatching rake brings the thatch layer to the surface. It makes a good addition to the compost.

Dividing Perennials

To keep your perennial plants performing at their peak, it's necessary to lift and divide most of them every few years, and early spring is a good time to do this. You'll end up with more plants than you started with, so begin a new flower bed or give the extras to a friend, local horticultural societies, or schools. As a last resort, the discards can go on the compost.

Some people prefer to divide their crowded perennials in the fall, but others find it, in the words of my friend Brian Bixley, "a risky business." As in so much of Canadian gardening, when you should do it depends on your zone. You have to be sure the plants will have enough time to get their roots growing well in the new place and that the new growth is not too tender to survive the winter. Spring offers the welcome combination of soft rains, warming soil, and mild—or at least milder—weather. Another advantage is that your flower beds are still just coming out of their winter sleep, and except for the bulbs, not much is in bloom, so you won't be upsetting a favourite colour combination. Later in the year, in August and September, lifting perennials for dividing can cause some gaps in otherwise attractive borders.

Some perennials have shallow roots, others have rather deep roots, and yet others have rhizomes—tuberlike roots. Many deep-taproot perennials don't take kindly to being disturbed, so lift and divide only those that are beginning to look crowded. Some perennials, such as astilbes and columbines, have a woody crown that needs to be divided carefully with a good sharp kitchen knife, making sure each division has both stems and roots.

This is a good time of year to divide perennials, such as this coreopsis. With a garden fork, loosen the soil and lift the plant.

After shaking soil off the roots, gently pry the roots apart.

The magic of gardening: now you've got two plants! Firm the soil around them in their new spot in the border and keep well watered.

Plan to divide perennials just when new growth is visible. Work with a shallow container of water at hand to keep the roots of the divisions moist as you proceed. Starting about 10 to 15 cm (4 to 6 inches) from the plant, loosen the soil and dig up the plant, using a garden fork and making sure you've got its root structure within the ball of soil. Shake off the soil, then inspect the plant for natural places to make cuts for the division. Look for new clusters of stems with their own roots. If you make only two or three divisions, your new plants will recover more quickly from this operation; on the other hand, if you want a larger yield and don't mind babying the new plants somewhat, you can make more divisions.

Some plants are trickier to divide because a natural place for the division is not apparent. Check the roots and try to match them with a section of stalks growing out of the crown (the point where roots and stems join and from which new shoots issue) to decide where to make the cut.

Using a sharp knife, prune away dead or damaged growth or roots and plant as you would a container-grown plant. None of this seemingly rough treatment will harm the plant. Keep the newly planted divisions well watered for the first few weeks and mulch them to help conserve the moisture. As with all mulch, don't let it touch the stems of the plants.

If you're feeling nervous about lifting and dividing, these plants are easily divided: yarrow, wormwood, aster, astilbe, bellflower, chrysanthemums, coreopsis, evening primrose, phlox, primrose, veronicas.

Long-Blooming Perennials

The goal of many gardeners is to have colour in the garden throughout the year or for as long as possible. Annuals spotted here and there in the beds will assure you both of colour and supplies of cut flowers, but perennials can also grace your garden with colour for many weeks.

Gardening centres will be setting out all manner of tempting plant material at this time of year. As you cruise the aisles, planning list in hand, give a thought to perennials that have extended blooming periods. The list that follows offers a selection of some versatile perennials, with notes about their care. To extend blooming periods, be religious about deadheading (see Chapter 6). Divide the plants every few years to continue getting good blooms.

Balloon Flower (*Platycodon*)

The buds on this plant are what gives it its odd name—they look like little blue, pink, or white balloons before they open. Balloon flower blooms from midsummer to frost, reaching a height of about 45 to 95 cm (18 to 36 inches). Its shoots can be slow to make an appearance in the spring, so it's a good practice to mark their location. It likes a slightly acid, well-drained soil in a sunny spot. It has long roots and doesn't like to be moved. To Zone 3.

Bergamot (*Monarda*)

You might know this plant by other names, such as bee balm and Oswego tea. It's not to everyone's liking—it can suffer from mildew, and its flowers and leaves are carried on the top half of the stem so it can look top-heavy. On the bright side, bees and hummingbirds love it, its fresh-smelling leaves make a pleasant tea, and its red, purple, or pink flowers can decorate a salad. Kept deadheaded, it blooms from July to frost. To prevent mildew, place it where the air circulates well; to help the lower stem fill out with leaves, give it a rich, moist soil. It will grow to 60 to 90 cm (2 to 3 feet). To Zone 4.

Blanket Flower (*Gaillardia*)

Keep deadheading blanket flower and it will bloom from June to August. Its daisylike flowers range from red to gold to brown; depending on the variety, it can grow to 90 cm (3 feet). It needs well-drained soil, and is a rather short-lived perennial. To Zone 5.

Coreopsis

Pinks can be tucked here and there at the front of a border or in a rock garden.

Coral Bells *(Heuchera)*

The white, red, or pink bell-shaped flowers bloom from July for more than two months. In zones 2 and 3, try 'Brandon Glow,' 'Brandon Pink,' and 'Northern Fire.' It will tolerate dry conditions but prefers moist well-drained soils, and will grow to 30 to 60 cm (1 to 2 feet). To Zone 2.

Coreopsis *(Coreopsis)*

Many varieties of coreopsis are available, but threadleaf coreopsis *(Coreopsis verticillata* 'Moonbeam') is a cheerful addition to the garden, and more delicate-looking than some of its relatives. It's a very successful coreopsis for the prairies. It flowers all summer and into fall, with small pale-yellow daisylike flowers and ferny foliage. To improve its blooming, cut back the spent flower stalks at the base. It needs full sun in soil with good drainage and will grow to 30 to 60 cm (1 to 2 feet). To Zone 4.

Cornflower *(Centaurea)*

The perennial cornflower (*C. montanta*) is not as brightly blue as the annual cornflower, but it is very hardy, even in poor soil, and easy to grow. This grey-leaved plant will reach a maximum of 50 cm (20 inches), likes sun, and will bloom from June through August. To Zone 2.

Cranesbill *(Geranium)*

Cranesbill is the true geranium, not the pelargoniums that are popularly called geraniums. 'Johnson's Blue' offers its beautiful blue blooms over the summer season. Some other suggestions: *G. cinereum* 'Ballerina' grows in a mound and has pale purple-pink flowers all summer; *G. himalayense* (several cultivars) has blue flowers, grows in clumps or as a ground cover, and likes morning sun. Heights vary from 30 to 60 cm (1 to 2 feet). Give them all well-drained soil and some winter protection. To Zone 4.

Foxglove *(Digitalis)*

Foxgloves are really biennials—you plant them one year, they flower the second year, then die. But I'm including them in the perennial section because they can have a reasonably long blooming time and I love the cottage-garden feel they give to a border. And although they die after their second year, they self-seed. Cut back their first bloom to encourage a second, which should not be cut back but left to go to seed. Foxgloves will grow in sun but do best in partial shade. Dwarf foxglove (*D. purpurea* 'Foxy') will grow to 90 cm (3 feet). The tubular blossoms are white, yellow, or red. 'Excelsior' hybrids will tower to 1.5 m (5 feet) and more; their flowers come in red, purple, pink, yellow, or white. To Zone 4.

Flax *(Linum perenne)*

Borne on graceful, arching 45 cm (18-inch) stems that sway in a gentle breeze, the delicate yellow or blue flax flowers drop their petals at the end of the day. The next day there'll be another lot of buds opening to the sun, and so it continues for most of the summer. They are self-seeders, so you will quickly have a gorgeous patch if you let them take hold. To Zone 5.

Geum (*Geum quellyon*)

Geums like coolish summers, making them perfect for northern gardens. Their cheerful yellow, orange, bronze, or scarlet flowers are somewhat like large, many-petalled buttercups. They don't mind a bit of shade, as long as the soil is moist and well drained. 'Mrs. Bradshaw' is a popular cultivar, with semidouble scarlet flowers that bloom from July to frost. To Zone 4.

Golden Marguerite (*Anthemis tinctoria*)

With bright-yellow flowers like small single mums, this prolific plant blooms from June to frost in milder regions; in zones 2 and 3 it's more likely to be August and September. Give it a hot, dry site; it will tolerate poor soil conditions. It can grow to 90 cm (3 feet). To Zone 2.

Pinks (*Dianthus*)

Grown in a rock garden or spreading along the front of a border, *D. alwoodii*, which comes in many colours, and *D. arenarius*, which comes in white with purple edges, are charming additions, blooming from June through to August or September. They prefer a light, well-drained alkaline soil and full sun. They'll reach 30 cm (1 foot), and if you prune back by a third after the first flowering, you'll have another round of blooms the same season. To Zone 4.

Purple flowers and grey-green foliage of salvia

Purple Coneflower (*Echinacea purpurea*)

Purple coneflower is easy to grow, and blooms from July to frost. It has dark-green leaves and brownish stems, and can reach 1.2 m (4 feet). To Zone 2.

Salvia (*Salvia superba*)

Perennial salvia has a lot going for it — it's drought-resistant, bugs don't bother it, and it blooms from June or July to the first hard frost. Related to sage, it carries purple flowers on grey-green foliage and grows to about 1.2 m (4 feet). Give it good drainage. To Zone 4.

Sea Holly (*Eryngium*)

Eryngiums are interesting thistlelike plants with prickly silvery leaves and silver-blue flower heads. *E. alpinum* will grow to 60 to 90 cm (2 to 3 feet), blooming from June to August. Use for summer cutting or in dried flower arrangements; if you're going to dry them, pick them before they have fully opened. Plant in full sun, in well-drained soil. To Zone 5.

Sedum (*Sedum*)

Throughout the summer and into autumn, *S.* 'Autumn Joy' offers a changing hue, from the bright-green of its flower buds in summer to pink and rose, then rust in late September or early October. Its 15 cm (6-inch) flower heads are carried on stems about 60 cm (2 feet) tall, and are attractive to butterflies. It likes full sun or light shade in well-drained soil of any type. Sedum is one of my favourite perennials because it blooms for such a long time (six to twelve weeks) and is a reliable performer from year to year. Another bonus is that it's insect- and disease-resistant. To Zone 2.

Plant thrift in rock gardens or tuck between paving stones to show it off.

Shasta Daisy (*Chrysanthemum* × *superbum*)

Like flax, Shasta daisies bring movement to the garden as their heads sway in a gentle summer breeze. They can grow to 90 cm (3 feet), producing their tall stalks from a dark-green clump of leaves. Pinching them back early in the season will make the plant bushier. Their cheerful yellow-and-white flowers — the traditional daisy — are good for cutting, and if you're consistent in keeping up with deadheading, you'll have blooms from June to August. When the plant seems to have finished blooming, cut the stalks back near the ground and you will be rewarded with another, smaller, flowering. They like sun and rich, well-drained soil, and lots of watering when it's dry. Try *C. maximum* in zones 2 and 3. To Zone 4.

Thrift (*Armeria*)

Both varieties described here do well in rock gardens, need full sun and well-drained soil, and will give you colour from June to September. *A. maritima* 'Alba' has white flowers that rise on tall straight stems to about 15 cm (6 inches); *A. maritima* 'Laucheana' grows to the same height but has deep pink flowers and does well in a seacoast garden. To Zone 2.

Valerian *(Centranthus)*

Red valerian, also known as Jupiter's beard, likes hot, dry situations. Its fleshy foliage is grey-green, and its flowers, which bloom from June to September, range from carmine to pink. It prefers sun but will tolerate partial shade, reaches about 75 cm (30 inches), and likes well-drained chalky soil. To Zone 4.

Yarrow *(Achillea)*

The pale-green feathery foliage of yarrows makes an attractive addition to the garden. Yarrows are easy to care for and have a preference for full sun and a well-drained soil. Fernleaf yarrow (*A. filipendulina* 'Cloth of Gold') has bright-yellow, long-lasting flower heads, and blooms from June through September. It can grow as tall as 90 cm (3 feet). Another long bloomer is sneezewort (*A. ptarmica* 'The Pearl'). It will produce tiny white buttonlike flowers from June through September. It grows to about 45 cm (18 inches). Be warned that it can become invasive. To Zone 2.

Purple coneflower (TOP); *yellow coneflower* (BELOW)

Yucca *(Yucca)*

Easy-to-grow yucca will give an exotic touch to your garden. The creamy-white bell-shaped flowers it throws up from its base of tall spiky leaves last for many weeks. Yuccas can grow as tall as 2 m (7 feet), are tolerant of heat and drought, and like a well-drained sandy or loamy soil. To Zone 4.

The Cold Frame Revisited

During April, you will be moving more seedlings to the cold frame or starting more seeds in the frame. At this time of year ventilation is essential—the cold frame needs careful watching, for temperatures inside the frame can escalate quickly and bake the tender seedlings. You might want to keep the lid off during the day.

Hardening-off: The seedlings that are flourishing by your windows or under your lighting system are ready to take another step. Up until now they have been treated like hothouse flowers, but it's necessary for them to get used to the environment they'll be growing in. They have to be hardened off—that is, acclimatized to the colder outdoors—by a stint in the cold frame.

The first candidates for the cold frame are those that will be transplanted out in the garden first, the cool-weather crops (see Chapter 5).

Choose a warm day to move your trays of seedlings out to the cold frame. During the day, keep the cover open to prevent the hot temperature from baking the tender seedlings. As well, the plants need to be exposed to some wind to start strengthening their stems and branches. In the evening, close the cover and, if the temperature is expected to drop, protect the cold frame with blankets, cardboard, or anything else that provides insulation.

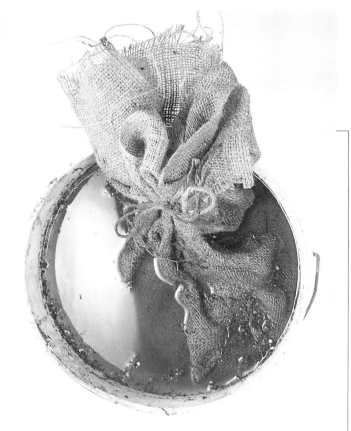

Compost Tea

"Teas" made from compost are good pick-me-ups for plants that are in need of help, such as young transplants in the cold frame. Plants in containers and hanging baskets will love it, too.

A tea can be made simply by mixing equal parts of compost and water in a bucket or watering can. Stir it now and then and leave it to "steep" for a couple of days. Then it's ready to use. You can make several batches of tea from the same compost. After you're done, put the compost back on the pile or dig it directly into the garden.

A larger quantity of tea can be brewed in a barrel or garbage can. Put the compost in a fabric bag of some sort—a burlap bag, an old pillowcase, or an old canvas shopping bag. Place the bag of compost in the can and fill with water. You can either hook the bag to the edge of the can or tie a rope around the bag, letting the rope hang over the edge. Stir the mixture every day, and in a week you'll have compost tea.

If you use a barrel with a spigot or tap at the bottom, you'll be able to siphon off your tea.

You can also make manure tea in the same fashion, substituting well-rotted manure for the compost.

If you have seedlings in flats or planted directly in the soil of the cold frame, about a week before you're ready to transplant them into the garden, root-prune the seedlings to help them avoid shock. This is a very simple procedure, and well worth it. Cut between the rows of seedlings with a sharp knife, as if you were cutting a cake. Be sure to cut to the bottom of the flat; if your seedlings are growing in the soil, make the cuts deep in the earth. Water the seedlings immediately. Each plant will develop new roots within its own cube of soil, making it much easier to transplant.

The cold frame is busy in April, as seedlings are hardened off. It can also act as a holding place for purchased flats.

Some other ways to harden off plants during mild spring days:

- Take the seed trays outdoors and place them in a shaded spot for a few hours. Do this every day, leaving them out for longer periods each day and gradually exposing them to more sun. Protect them from the wind.
- A garage provides a sheltered spot for hardening off seedlings.
- A small A-frame lath structure can be placed over seedling trays to protect them from the harsh elements outside.

Kids' Gardening:
Vegetables

If your child has shown interest in how and why things grow, build on that interest by setting aside a patch for his or her garden. You already know what your child's attention span is, and even if you've seen enthusiasms wane quickly, don't let this put you off. You might have to do some (or all) of the watering, weeding, and mulching—but your youngster will likely be there when it's time to harvest!

Kids like to see fast results, so here are some plants that will grow quickly, for fairly immediate gratification, and some that take longer but will provide fun months later. Start the seeds indoors or plant them out in the garden when the soil has warmed up. (For more detailed cultivation information, see the vegetable list in Chapter 5.)

Beans: This rewarding crop has a lot going for it where kids are concerned. The seeds are easy to handle because they're fairly large and growth is quite quick.

Carrots: Carrot seeds are small, so kids will probably need help planting.

Lettuce: Another easy-to-grow vegetable with fairly small seeds. You can try several varieties of lettuce to see the differences in colour, leaf shape, and taste, for example.

Ornamental gourds: These will really pay off in the late summer when the kids see some of the fantastic and colourful shapes. After harvesting the gourds, wash them with a 10:1 solution of water and bleach, dry, leave in warm place for several months, then coat with paste wax or clear shellac when seeds rattle.

Peas: Fresh peas can be a real eye-opener to anyone, and they're an especially rewarding crop for kids.

Potatoes: There's something about growing potatoes that's appealing to adults as well as to kids. Perhaps it's the idea of buried treasure. One of my fondest memories is digging potatoes with my daughter. Her eyes were like saucers as we unearthed one potato after another. Be warned, though, that potatoes take up a lot of garden space.

Pumpkins: This is another crop that can take up a fair amount of room—but it's fun to grow your own jack-o'-lantern. The plot should be about 2 m (6 feet) square, and even then, don't be surprised if the pumpkin tries to escape.

Radishes: Even if your child doesn't like radishes, they make good seeds for a child's garden because they are ready for harvesting so quickly.

Sunflowers: Fun to look at, and a feast for birds later in the season, sunflowers can sometimes seem like the beanstock in *Jack and the Beanstalk*.

Tomatoes: Your child might be surprised at all the tomato choices available—cherry tomatoes to eat like candy, plum tomatoes for spaghetti sauce, and regular tomatoes for slicing into sandwiches and salads.

An important piece of advice for gardening with kids: try to avoid too many rules. If they don't want to plant the seeds in rows, don't worry. You can tell them the advantages of spacing the seeds as they plant them, but this is their garden, and as you know, a garden is a personal thing.

April Gardening Checklist

General

🌱 Start to feed houseplants on a monthly basis. Prune and/or repot overgrown household plants.

Ornamental Garden

🌱 Remove winter mulch.

🌱 Continue to lift and divide perennials. Plant new perennials.

🌱 Root cuttings of geraniums from plants that you repotted in February.

🌱 Rake and fertilize lawn. If crab grass was a problem, apply a fertilizer that contains crab-grass preventer.

🌱 Plant deciduous and coniferous trees and shrubs.

🌱 Take root cuttings for propagation (see Chapter 9) and layer shrubs for propagating.

🌱 Pot up canna lilies.

Zones 2 to 6

🌱 Take winter covering off roses.

🌱 Plant shrubs, trees, and hedge material.

🌱 Harden off and plant out pansy seedlings started in January.

Zones 7 to 9

🌱 Deadhead daffodils. Leave foliage.

🌱 Finish rose pruning.

🌱 Prune shrubs that have finished flowering.

🌱 Sow more hardy annuals outdoors.

Fruit and Vegetable Garden

🌱 Plant fruit trees.

🌱 Lightly side-dress asparagus and rhubarb with compost or well-rotted manure.

Zones 2 to 6

🌱 Start preparing vegetable beds as soon as soil is workable. Spread compost or well-rotted manure on vegetable bed. If cover crops were sown, turn them under. Wait two weeks before preparing beds and sowing new crops.

🌱 Seed outdoors cool-weather vegetables such as onions, peas, radishes, and spinach (see Chapter 5 for other hardy vegetables) as soon as soil is workable and bed is prepared.

🌱 Start broccoli seeds indoors.

🌱 Start to harden off and transplant seedlings, beginning with lettuce.

Zones 7 to 9

🌱 Start outdoor sowing of potatoes, green onions, cabbage, and leeks in first half of month; in second half of month, beets, carrots, broccoli, cauliflower, Swiss chard, parsnip, kale, and lettuce.

🌱 Transplant vegetables from cold frame.

🌱 Use row covers to protect transplants from insect pests and unexpected frost.

Chapter 5

May

Get Growing

This is a busy month in the garden, for both plants and people. If you're pushing your microclimate to its limits in order to extend the gardening season and get earlier results, you're going to need to protect those plants occasionally. There are some time-honoured ways of doing so, as well as some more recent ideas and products.

Protecting Your Plants

Even though the early plants you've transplanted from the cold frame to the garden are fairly hardy, they're still susceptible to frost. By adapting the principle of the cold frame, however, you can offer protection to these plants either individually or in rows. You might want to try some of these ideas just to give your plants a good start and not just when frost threatens. You'll want to use these techniques again in the fall, when frosts threaten the crops you've nurtured all summer long.

Cloches and hot caps: Cloches and hot caps are individual minigreenhouses that you can buy or make yourself. They are used overnight in the spring and fall to protect vegetables seedlings and tender perennials from sudden frosts. The purchased ones are made of translucent waxed paper, fibreglass, or plastic and may be pointed or rounded. Some have a ventilation hole in the top to prevent severe heat buildup. If you prefer, you can make your own from a large plastic jug. Just cut off the bottom, place the jug over the plant, and secure with a small stake driven through the handle. Remove the lid as needed for ventilation. It's possible to make cloches from glass jugs, but this is more difficult and requires greater care, since you need to use glass-cutting tools.

Other discarded household items can also be pressed into service. Start looking around and you'll see lots of potential cloches — plastic ice-cream containers, pails, bowls, plastic dishpans, plastic pop bottles, even opaque plastic bags. If you plan to leave them on during a particularly cold day, don't forget to punch a few holes for ventilation.

Such season extenders work well on tomatoes, eggplants, and peppers when they're still fairly young. As the plants get larger, you could make portable frames for individual vegetables, covering the sides and top with plastic sheeting. The plastic sheeting itself, however, may not offer enough frost protection, but it can be supplemented with blankets or quilts.

Rule of Thumb

A few days before setting out your transplants, warm up the soil by putting out the cloches over the spots where the individual plants will go. A black plastic sheet spread over the soil will also warm it up, but be sure to use some stones to weigh down the sheet. I learned the hard way that a few minutes of strong wind will ruin all my good intentions.

Two faces of gardening: the work and the rewards.

The tomato plant enclosed by this Wall o' Water is kept warm on cool nights.

The benefits of this treatment are seen in the lush foliage of a plant that has grown out of its protection.

Light fabric row covers protect vegetables from insect invasions while allowing moisture and light in. Eventually, as the plants grow larger, the covers will have to be removed, but the plants will have had a good start.

Hot caps are small domes made of opaque, porous, usually waxed paper, which provides better cold protection than clear plastic, but does not allow as much light in. They are useful for protecting tender seedlings from cold winds. Commercial hot caps are available, or you can make your own from newspaper by folding it to create a hat — something you might have done as a child. Anchor hot caps with a rock or other heavy object so they don't blow away on a windy day.

Wall o' Water: This is the brand name of an ingenious solar-heated plant protector that's frequently used on tomatoes. It's a ring of open-ended plastic tubes, which stands about 45 cm (18 inches) high. Place it around the plant and fill the tubes with water. The water gives the ring enough support for it to stand up. During the day the water warms up, and during the night the heat is released. Heat retention and protection for the plant can be increased by tilting the tubes inward, leaving only a small opening at the top.

Plastic tents: Erect a tent over a bed of tender plants to protect them from harsh winds and conserve heat. Such a structure operates like a cold frame, except on a larger scale. Because planting is often more intensive on raised beds, tents that cover the entire bed are more appropriate than a bunch of small cloches.

The tent can be made by erecting a ridge pole, across which plastic sheeting is draped. Alternatives are to build a frame of wood or plastic or aluminum pipe over the bed (the frame can have square corners or be arched) or to use a V-shaped pea-vine support. Fitted over the frame or support are 4 mil plastic sheets that have openings at both ends for ventilation. The plastic on these frames has to be anchored around the edges with bricks, boards, soil, or stones so it doesn't blow away on windy days.

The tent is used only in the spring and fall to help the soil heat up, encouraging the plants to grow more quickly. The covering should be removed when flowers appear on the plants so that pollination can occur.

Plastic tunnels: To make a plastic tunnel, you need hoops (you can make your own — details follow), which are then placed over a row or rows of seedlings; plastic is thrown over the hoops and anchored along the length by soil, planks, bricks, or other heavy objects.

Vine crops such as cucumbers, melons, pumpkins, and squash do well in a tunnel. In areas where the soil takes a long time to warm up, a combination of plastic mulch and tunnels or tents will get your heat-loving plants off to a good start. Once the plants have put on good growth, remove the tunnel. (If your plants start to wilt or look burned, it's a sign that the plastic has to come off.) As with the tent I just described, the cover must be removed when flowers appear for pollination.

Hoops can be made of wire about 2 m (6½ feet) long. Bend the pieces of wire into a U shape and stick them in the ground in a row, about 2 m (6½ feet) apart. The two end hoops should be reinforced by placing two of the hoops closely together, about 30 cm (1 foot) apart. Arrange the clear plastic over the hoops, either fixing the ends so that they can be opened easily to allow air to circulate, or folding the ends and anchoring them or staking them in the soil. If you choose the latter, you will need to make some slits in the top of the cover to allow excessive heat to escape.

Row covers can cut off access to your plants, so keep this in mind as you place them. It might be more of a nuisance to make several short tunnels rather than one long one, but it will be easier to open the ends and see how the entire row is doing, as well as to water when necessary. Another option is to slit the plastic at intervals along the top of the tunnel or buy plastic that is already slit. This allows for ventilation, and makes it possible to reach into the tunnel from the top.

Floating row covers: These are similar to the tunnels described earlier, but the cover is a very lightweight fabric, and sits on the plants, rather than being attached to a frame. This makes it easy to apply to the garden, to store, and to move around. The fabric is porous and allows water, light, and air to reach the plants. It will need to be anchored to the soil, however. If you're covering a newly planted bed with a floating row cover, you'll want to use something, such as a series of small sticks, to hold it off the soil to give the plants room to grow. Keep your eye out for insects if the fabric isn't firmly anchored all around. Unfortunately, the protection provides an attractive environment for insects as well as plants.

Used Tires Extend the Season

A used rubber tire can have a special place in the vegetable garden, especially if you want to grow heat-loving cucumbers, melons, pumpkins, or zucchini. They'll all take off in a tire.

In the early spring, fill the tire with a rich soil-and- compost mixture. Sow the seed just after the risk of frost has passed. The tire will draw daytime heat and radiate it at night, warming the planting soil quickly and evenly. Leave the tire in place all summer and you'll have an extra-early crop.

Rule of Thumb

Homemade sun traps: Pile hay around three sides of heat-loving plants to give them a good start. The open side should face south. During cold snaps in the spring and fall, cover it with plastic to further conserve heat and protect.

Heavier row covers offer some frost protection, but can overheat. Lighter covers are often used to protect plants from insects (when the edges are firmly sealed all around). With care, you can give your heat-loving plants an early start by using very lightweight floating row covers in combination with plastic mulch (see Chapter 6). Even so, you will have to watch out for overheating. Experiment with several weights and combinations to see what works best for your conditions and the plants you want to grow. Like the tent and tunnel, the covers will have to be removed for pollination.

Row covers are sold under various brand names; two of the best-known are Reemay and Agronet.

Emergency frost protectors: If you haven't any of the devices described earlier at hand, you can use a variety of other household objects when frost threatens. They really are better for emergency situations than as everyday protectors. Keep old sheets, blankets, towels, or thin rugs handy to drape over climbing plants. Smaller seedlings can be covered with such things as inverted flowerpots, pails, cardboard boxes, and baskets. Even newspaper can be used as protection in a pinch. Run a line attached to stakes at either end of the row and pin the newspapers to it in a tentlike fashion. Secure the edges with soil, planks, bricks, or anything else that is heavy. Cover the plants in the late afternoon—if you wait too long, the soil and air will have begun to cool off. Remove all these protectors the next morning so the plants don't get overheated.

Getting the Most from Your Vegetable Plot

When you were planning your garden and ordering your seeds, you also had to figure out when to sow the seeds. Naturally, you're interested in getting plants going quickly and knowing how to keep them producing for as long as possible in your particular climate. In order to get the best yield, you'll need to know whether the vegetable likes cool or warm weather, when the crop will be harvested, special requirements of the plant, potential insect and disease problems (see chapters 6 and 7 for treatment methods), and watering needs. This information will help you make the best use of your resources so you can get the healthiest, lushest produce possible.

Some vegetables can be interplanted—that is, a fast-growing vegetable and a slower-growing vegetable are planted in the same row or bed so that you can harvest the faster-growing vegetable while the slower-growing one is just beginning to fill out. In other cases, you'll take out spent plants and replace them with sowings of new plants that will be harvested later in the season. Check out Chapter 7 for some hints about vegetables to start indoors, so they'll be ready to plant out in July or August for fall harvesting.

Don't forget about crop rotation—some plants don't like to be planted where they grew last year. (I've noted such plants in the following list.) See pages 127 to 129 for information about succession planting, crop rotation, and companion planting—plants that like each other!

I have occasionally mentioned dates, but they are guidelines only—be sure to check your local conditions. All the vegetables listed do best in full sun unless otherwise noted. Also, the watering suggestions give the prime times to water if Mother Nature hasn't been cooperating.

Plan your planting and harvesting dates to ensure continuous use of your plot. Corn (FOREGROUND ABOVE) will need a whole season to reach maturity, but the beans beyond can be replaced with a late vegetable after harvesting. The carrots (BELOW) can also be replaced after an early harvest with another sowing.

Rule of Thumb

For most crops, picking frequently will give better and longer yields.

Crops with fine small seeds often need to be thinned — lettuce, carrots, beets, radishes, for example — but you can avoid this chore by mixing these fine seeds with dry sand. Sow the seeds with sand and you'll get a more even, well-spaced crop.

Cool-Weather Crops

Let's start with the cool-weather crops, since they're the first seeds you sow and the first seedlings you set out; they will provide the first harvests.

Cool-weather crops can be planted out early in the season and can tolerate some frost, as long as it's a light one.

Beets

SOIL: Cool, moist, well-worked (loose) soil. Like a nearly neutral pH.

SOWING TIME: Sow three to four weeks before last frost or start indoors. Sow successively to July or August.

FERTILIZING NEEDS: Light feeder. Do well with a seaweed fertilizer.

WATERING NEEDS: Water only when soil starts to dry out.

PESTS AND DISEASES: Flea beetles sometimes munch small holes in the leaves, which retards the plant's growth. Treat with rotenone.

HARVESTING: Pick the greens of beets as well as the root — the tops have more vitamins. You can also mulch beets heavily and leave them in the bed for the winter and spring harvesting.

COMMENTS:

- Light frost will not harm the young plants.
- Keep well weeded.
- Grow baby varieties of beets in containers.

Broad Beans

SOIL: Cool soil.

SOWING TIME: Sow early — end of April to end of May. Plant a second crop in the late summer in mild climates.

FERTILIZING NEEDS: Medium feeder.

WATERING NEEDS: Water when plants begin to bloom and when pods start to develop. Carry on with watering through harvest period.

PESTS AND DISEASES: Prone to rust, though rust-resistant varieties (noted in seed catalogues) are available. Control aphids with insecticidal soap.

HARVESTING: They're ready for picking when you can see the outline of the bean through the pod, which should be about 5 to 8 cm (2 to 3 inches) long.

COMMENTS:

- Fixes nitrogen in the soil. When beans are finished, don't pull up the roots; leave them to return the nitrogen to the soil as they decompose.
- Young plants can withstand a light frost.
- Matures later than other beans but will age quickly in hot weather.
- Pinch out growing tip for a better crop and denser growth.
- Rotate bean crops at least every three years.

Broccoli

SOIL: Cool, fertile, loose soil, but also tolerant of fairly heavy clay. Avoid soil in which another member of the cabbage family was planted the previous two years.

SOWING TIME: Start indoors from seed six or seven weeks before the last frost or sow outdoors during the two weeks before and after the last frost. Seedlings go out in late April. Mulch with straw or leaf mould when soil is warm.

FERTILIZING NEEDS: A medium to heavy feeder that benefits from additions of nitrogen. Every two weeks fertilize with manure tea or fish emulsion.

WATERING NEEDS: Water well and regularly throughout the season, since broccoli is a shallow-rooted plant and thus dries out quickly.

PESTS AND DISEASES: Seedlings can be attacked by root maggots; lay newspaper, cardboard, or tar paper around seedlings. Control flea beetles with rotenone. Cutworms can be forestalled by placing collars around seedlings. Try planting chives and garlic nearby as insect repellents.

HARVESTING: Pick during coolest part of day. Smaller shoots are produced once the main head is cut, so you can keep harvesting broccoli often into the fall. Harvest frequently when the weather is warm.

COMMENTS:

❧ Young plants can tolerate light frost, but seedlings should be protected.

❧ Plant in spring through July for successive harvesting.

Carrots

SOIL: Cool, loose, deep, sandy soil. Prefer a pH of about 6.5.

SOWING TIME: Sow direct in soil up to five weeks before last frost. Plant weekly until mid-June, thinning as needed. Seed can be slow to germinate.

FERTILIZING NEEDS: Light feeder. Mulch in warm weather to keep soil cool.

WATERING NEEDS: Water well and frequently, especially in the weeks after seeds have been planted and during dry spells.

PESTS AND DISEASES: Few pests and diseases threaten carrots. If yours are bothered by the carrot rust fly, use row covers to protect the plants and work in the carrot patch on still evenings.

Purple flowering broccoli

Carrots and beets — two cool-weather crops

HARVESTING: Thin seedlings and use in salads. My friend Lois Hole, who gardens on the prairies, stores carrots outdoors in a plastic pail sunk into a hole in the garden. Covered with a layer of newspaper, they will keep until Christmas, she says.

COMMENTS:

- Weed well; carrots will not be able to stand up to weeds if left untended.
- Flavour improves with a light frost.
- Good for container growing — just make sure the container is at least 25 cm (10 inches) deep.
- Plant a second crop in October for harvesting early the following spring. Sow the seeds thickly and twice as deep as for a spring planting. You should be able to harvest these carrots two to four weeks earlier than a spring-planted crop.

Cauliflower

SOIL: Cool, rich, well-drained soil. Likes sweet (alkaline) soil, so you may need to add lime. Avoid soil in which another member of the cabbage family was planted the previous two or three years.

SOWING TIME: Start seed indoors six to eight weeks before last frost date. Plant out when danger of frost has passed. For fall harvesting, sow seed about two and a half months before first frost.

FERTILIZING NEEDS: Heavy feeder.

WATERING NEEDS: Water well when heads are developing. Mulch heavily when plants are about 10 cm (4 inches) to conserve moisture in the soil.

PESTS AND DISEASES: Seedlings can be attacked by root maggots; prevent by laying newspaper, cardboard, or tar paper around seedlings. Control flea beetles with rotenone. To head off cutworms, place collars around seedlings. Control cabbageworm with *Bacillus thuringiensis*. Try planting chives and garlic as insect repellents.

HARVESTING: Best to harvest when heads are small, compact, and firm. Retain outer leaves for storage.

COMMENTS:

- Difficult to grow.
- Cauliflower doesn't do well in frost, but needs cool weather to form a head.
- To keep the heads white, tie the leaves around the head and harvest a few days later.
- The plants mature quickly in very hot weather and do not form heads.

Garlic

SOIL: Cool, well-drained soil. Avoid planting where garlic or other onions were grown the previous season.

SOWING TIME: Late August is the best time to plant for harvesting the next summer. In cold zones, mulch over the winter. Can also be planted in spring, up to five weeks before last frost.

FERTILIZING NEEDS: Light feeder, but give a high-nitrogen fertilizer in the spring.

WATERING NEEDS: Water regularly when bulbs are growing.

PESTS AND DISEASES: Virtually none.

HARVESTING: Harvest in August when soil is quite dry.

COMMENTS:

- Good for container growing.
- Frost will not hurt garlic.
- Garlic needs a period of dormancy in temperatures below 18°C (64°F).
- Keep well weeded.
- Garlic is reputed to be an insect repellent. Try interplanting with other crops.
- Leave dried tops on garlic when harvesting. Braid the tops and hang for storage.

Dried garlic

*Two types of lettuce:
(ABOVE) head lettuce; (RIGHT)
leaf lettuce*

Leeks

SOIL: Cool, rich soil.

SOWING TIME: Start indoors in February or March; harden off seedlings in cold frame in April; transplant mid-May. If sowing outdoors, plant as soon as ground can be worked.

FERTILIZING NEEDS: Light to medium feeder.

WATERING NEEDS: Water deeply during dry spells.

PESTS AND DISEASES: Fairly disease- and pest-free.

HARVESTING: Dig up, roots and all, in August to October. In mild zones, mulch heavily to help them overwinter outdoors.

COMMENTS:

❧ Easy to grow.

❧ Keep well weeded.

❧ Can withstand light frosts, but it's better to protect them with mulch.

❧ To achieve the white stem, mound soil over the base as the plant grows.

Lettuce

SOIL: Cool, rich, well-drained soil.

SOWING TIME: Start indoors in March or sow outdoors when soil can be worked; seeds will germinate even in quite cool temperatures; sow every week or so; some lettuces will take more heat than others, so check the information on the seed packet carefully. I recommend mulching with straw, old hay, or dry grass clippings spread thinly.

FERTILIZING NEEDS: Medium feeder; fertilize with 6-12-12 when growing strongly.

WATERING NEEDS: Head lettuce needs frequent watering.

PESTS AND DISEASES: Spread diatomaceous earth around the plants to prevent slug damage.

HARVESTING: Harvest leaf lettuce by cutting off at soil level to encourage a second growth.

COMMENTS:

❧ A short-season plant, so good for interplanting with other crops.

❧ Leaf lettuce can be grown in a container, matures quickly, and tolerates partial shade.

❧ Bitter taste is the result of stress, so it's important to mulch and water consistently.

Onions

SOIL: Cool, moist, fertile, well drained soil.

SOWING TIME: Plant as early as possible; seedlings will not be harmed by light frosts. Sets of Spanish onions can be planted in late fall for harvesting the following spring and summer.

FERTILIZING NEEDS: Light feeder.

WATERING NEEDS: Keep well watered, but stop watering when tops fall.

PESTS AND DISEASES: Onion root maggot can attack roots; early mulching will provide a barrier; pull up and destroy infected roots. Sets are less likely to be affected by root maggots.

HARVESTING: Harvest when leaves have turned yellow.

COMMENTS:

❧ Spanish onions need a long growing season.

❧ If your soil is dry, mulch to keep weeds down; don't mulch if your soil tends to be damp.

Parsnips

SOIL: Cool, deep (30 cm/1 foot), loose soil.

SOWING TIME: Sow succession plantings five weeks before last frost until early June.

FERTILIZING NEEDS: Light feeders.

WATERING NEEDS: Will germinate in about three weeks; keep soil well watered during this time. Thereafter water only when soil is quite dry.

Onions waiting to be harvested

PESTS AND DISEASES: Virtually none.

HARVESTING: Leave in ground until late in fall for good flavour. In fact, they can be left in the ground — mulched heavily — over the winter and will have a sweeter taste; once the weather warms up in the spring parsnips will become woody.

COMMENTS:

❦ An easy-to-grow, slow-growing vegetable.

Peas

SOIL: Cool, rich, well-drained, moist soil. Peas shouldn't be planted in the same ground two years in a row.

SOWING TIME: Sow four weeks before last frost or as soon as ground can be worked. Sow second planting three to four weeks after the first. Mulch with dried grass clippings, straw, partially rotted leaves.

FERTILIZING NEEDS: Medium feeder. Fertilize with 6-2-12 when 15 to 20 cm (6 to 8 inches) tall or with superphosphate and kelp meal; look for low nitrogen number or you'll get too much foliage.

WATERING NEEDS: Water deeply if weather has been dry, especially when plants are starting to flower and fruit.

PESTS AND DISEASES: Virtually none, but if aphids appear, they can be controlled with insecticidal soap.

HARVESTING: Don't damage vines when picking — use scissors if necessary. Regular picking encourages more production. Pick shelling peas and snap peas when the pods are well rounded. Pick snow peas when pods are still flat. I'm sure that, just like mine, many readers' earliest memories of a vegetable garden include picking and eating peas straight off the vine — and kids don't like vegetables!

COMMENTS:

❦ Larger crops can be had from tall varieties, but dwarf varieties don't need trellising.

Snow peas

🌱 Peas can take some frost until they put forth blossoms.

🌱 Pea roots from spent plants add nitrogen to the soil. When cleaning the bed where peas grew, don't pull up the roots. Let them stay and release their nitrogen to benefit the crop that will be planted there next year.

Potatoes

SOIL: Cool, light, well-drained soil. Do not plant in alkaline soil or where potatoes, tomatoes, eggplants, or peppers (all members of the same family) were planted the previous two years. Potatoes benefit from being planted where peas or beans grew the year before.

SOWING TIME: Plant about two weeks before last killing frost. Mulch with plastic where season is short.

FERTILIZING NEEDS: Heavy feeder. Apply 6-12-12 monthly.

WATERING NEEDS: Water regularly, especially in hot, dry spells.

PESTS AND DISEASES: Larvae of the Colorado potato beetle eat the foliage. The egg clusters are a recognizable bright orange and are found on the underside of the leaves. Treat the orange larvae with rotenone. Their adult beetles are black-and-orange striped, and can be picked off the plant.

HARVESTING: Dig when potatoes are large enough to eat — anywhere from the peak blossom time until the plant top completely collapses. If you're not sure they're ready, pull back the soil to see the size of the potatoes. You can harvest a few potatoes and leave the rest to grow.

COMMENTS:

🌱 Get a bigger crop by piling earth around the shoots as they grow, but not when they are in bloom. This practice also helps keep the soil cool.

Potato plants — buried treasure!

Radishes — ready for eating!

❧ Leave the foliage on the plant after flowering. It is still working to produce food for the potatoes. Cut off the foliage and stems in late August or September, then dig up the crop a couple of weeks later. This will result in potatoes that store better.

❧ Sometimes when potatoes are growing quickly they will appear on the surface of the soil and turn green where exposed, which indicates they are developing solanine, a poisonous substance. Don't eat any of these potatoes with green, but save them for next year's seed.

Radishes

SOIL: Cool, rich, moist, well-drained soil.

SOWING TIME: Sow seeds frequently, starting about five weeks before last frost and on to mid-July, as long as the weather is not too hot. They will not perform well in extremely hot weather.

FERTILIZING NEEDS: Light feeder.

WATERING NEEDS: Keep well watered or radishes will become woody.

PESTS AND DISEASES: Seedlings can be attacked by root maggots; prevent by laying newspaper, cardboard, or tar paper around seedlings. Control flea beetles with rotenone and cutworms with collars placed around seedlings. Try planting chives and garlic nearby as insect repellents.

HARVESTING: Pick when they have reached their full size, which can be as soon as three weeks after planting. If you leave them in the ground too long, they will attract root maggots and will also become woody.

COMMENTS:

❧ Good for interplanting, since radishes are a short-season crop.

Spinach

SOIL: Cool, rich, well-drained soil.

SOWING TIME: As soon as soil can be worked; sow at three-week intervals up to the middle of May. Seeds will germinate at 4°C (40°F). Subsequent sowings can be made in July, August, or September for late-fall harvesting. Thin seedlings several times.

FERTILIZING NEEDS: Medium feeder; needs nitrogen, especially in sandy soil.

WATERING NEEDS: Water well in a dry spring.

PESTS AND DISEASES: Cutworm can be a problem; treat with *Bacillus thuringiensis*; flea beetles sometimes appear — prevent by using a floating row cover for the first few weeks after growth appears.

HARVESTING: Harvest in June, freeing up space for a heat-loving crop.

COMMENTS:

❧ Spinach absolutely does not like hot weather, which causes it to bolt to seed.

❧ The plant will tolerate some shade.

❧ Picking individual leaves rather than whole plant will extend the harvest.

❧ Good for container growing.

❧ For an early-spring treat in mild zones, seed spinach in the early fall, mulch, and harvest in the spring; or sow in cold frame.

Warm-Weather Crops

Warm-weather crops are those that will not generally tolerate frost when first seeded or planted out as seedlings. They are planted out later than cold weather crops, after the danger of frost has passed. But if you're looking to extend your season, warm the soil with plastic sheets or individual cloches; protect seedlings with row covers, cloches, or hot caps—it's worth trying, but cross your fingers!

It's hard to believe that this bounteous growth came from a few seeds planted only a short time ago.

Beans, Green and Wax

SOIL: Warm, well-drained soil. Rotate beans at least every three years to avoid problems with disease.

SOWING TIME: Sow outdoors just before last frost until end of July. To encourage faster germination, soak the seeds overnight. If you live in an area with a very short season, you might want to start beans indoors to plant out four weeks after the last frost date.

FERTILIZING NEEDS: Medium feeder.

WATERING NEEDS: Water when plants begin to bloom and when pods start to develop.

PESTS AND DISEASES: Prone to rust, so plant rust-resistant varieties. Treat Mexican bean beetles with rotenone, pyrethrum, or Trounce liquid. Marigolds planted nearby will repel the beetle, as well.

HARVESTING: Pick when pods are tender and about the thickness of a pencil.

COMMENTS:

- Pick frequently to extend production.
- Susceptible to frost, so take care not to plant too early.
- In cool climates, mulch with plastic or use cloches for bush varieties. They will stop growing at temperatures lower than 10°C (50°F).
- Never work with beans—weeding or picking, for example—when the plants are damp; they are very susceptible to disease in that condition.

Beans, Pole

SOIL: Warm, well-drained soil.

SOWING TIME: Sow just before last frost until end of July. Provide something for plants to climb on.

FERTILIZING NEEDS: Feed with 6-12-12 once a month.

WATERING NEEDS: Water frequently, especially after flowering, for good production.

PESTS AND DISEASES: Can be prone to rust; plant rust-resistant varieties. Treat with garden sulphur.

HARVESTING: Same as for green and wax beans.

COMMENTS:

- Allow some beans to mature on the plant at the end of the harvest. Save them for sowing in subsequent seasons.

Bush beans

Brussels Sprouts

SOIL: Warm, fertile soil. Avoid soil in which a member of the cabbage family was planted the previous two years.

SOWING TIME: Sow seeds or transplant seedlings about one or two weeks before the last frost.

FERTILIZING NEEDS: Heavy feeder in sandy soil.

WATERING NEEDS: Watering can be cut back when the plant is established.

PESTS AND DISEASES: Root maggot can attack the plant. Mulch the soil with newspaper, getting as close to the plant as possible without touching the stem. Otherwise, use Diazinon. Cutworms also like Brussels sprouts; protect seedlings with cutworm collars.

HARVESTING: Pick in fall to late winter, depending on the severity of your climate, when the sprouts are firm and solid. Bottom sprouts mature first. If temperature falls below freezing before you've been able to harvest all the sprouts, dig or pull up whole plants and plant them in tubs of soil or damp sand in your basement. You should be able to continue to harvest them for another three or four weeks.

COMMENTS:

- Slow grower, so interplant with lettuce, arugula, radishes, or spinach to get the most out of your garden space.
- Taste better after a few light frosts.
- Although Brussels sprouts can't be started as early as cool-weather vegetables, they grow best in a cool, wet climate and do not do well in intense heat.
- In mid-September, pinch out the central growing tip so the upper sprouts will grow more quickly.

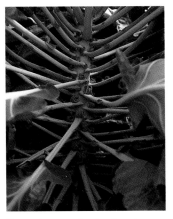

Brussels sprouts starting to form on the main stem

Cabbage

Cabbage

SOIL: Warm, rich, well-drained soil. Avoid soil in which another member of the cabbage family was planted the previous two years.

SOWING TIME: For early varieties, sow indoors five to eight weeks before last frost date. Transplant seedlings one or two weeks before last frost date. For late varieties, sow indoors or in cold frame around the last frost date; transplant in four to six weeks for fall harvesting.

FERTILIZING NEEDS: Top-dress with bone meal at planting time, about 30 mL (2 tablespoons) per plant, then use 10-10-10 every month.

WATERING NEEDS: Water well, especially when heads are developing.

PESTS AND DISEASES: Cutworms, root maggots, caterpillars, slugs, earwigs can be dispatched with rotenone. Other ways to deal with root maggots: mulch the soil with newspaper, getting as close to the plant as possible without touching the stem; or use Diazinon.

HARVESTING: The later in the season a variety matures, the better it will keep.

COMMENTS:

- Can withstand some frost; small plants are easy to protect from frost with cloches.

Corn

SOIL: Warm, fertile soil with good drainage. Don't plant in soil that had a corn crop the previous year. Best site is one where beans or peas were planted the year before.

SOWING TIME: Sow indoors four weeks before last frost. Plant out after last frost in blocks of at least five plants each way for assured pollination. Or sow outside, four to a hill, and thin to two after germination.

FERTILIZING NEEDS: Heavy feeder. Needs a fertilizer high in nitrogen and potassium.

WATERING NEEDS: Water well, especially when tassels and ears are being formed.

PESTS AND DISEASES: The corn borer, dirty-white worm with pinky or brown stripes, can cause plants to fall over and ears to drop; cobs and stalks will be wormy and the tassels will be broken. Control the pest with rotenone or pyrethrum. The corn earthworm, a large light-green or dark striped caterpillar, causes the tip of cob to become wormy and mouldy. Spray with insecticidal soap, or use *Bacillus thuringiensis* or pyrethrum, and be scrupulous about cleaning up cornstalks at the end of the harvest. Try planting onions and chives nearby to act as natural repellents. If raccoons are a problem, try leaving on a string of lights over the patch at night.

HARVESTING: Harvest about eighteen to twenty-four days after the silks have shown. For the best taste, pick just before you're ready to cook it. Nothing compares!

COMMENTS:

- Use plastic mulch to warm the soil before planting.
- Plant on the north or east side of a garden so that it will not shade lower-growing crops.
- Weed well. Roots are shallow, so don't cultivate deeply.
- Susceptible to frost; be prepared to protect it.
- Use a commercially available crow repellent on corn seed if crows are a problem in your area.

Cucumber

SOIL: Warm soil in a sheltered spot.

SOWING TIME: Sow seed indoors a month before last frost date or directly outside in hills in warm weather. Protect plants on cool nights.

FERTILIZING NEEDS: Use a starter fertilizer such as 10-52-10 weekly for three weeks; thereafter give extra compost and dried seaweed, if available, throughout the season.

WATERING NEEDS: Water thoroughly after sowing seeds, while flowers and fruit are being produced, and during dry spells.

PESTS AND DISEASES: Susceptible to diseases held in the soil—try to keep water off foliage and prevent soil from splashing on foliage. Don't do any cultivating or harvesting when the plants are wet or damp, such as first thing in the morning. If the leaves and stems suddenly wilt, squash vine borers are attacking your cucumbers. You will see a hole in the stem, which is their entry point. Just above this hole, dig for larva with a knife and flick out with your finger.

HARVESTING: Cut fruit from vines with a sharp knife to avoid damaging the plant.

COMMENTS:

- Plants are either bush or vining. Choose the one that best suits your site.
- Susceptible to frost; protect in northern gardens.

ABOVE:
Cucumber growing in a container
LEFT:
A delightful garden: some flowers, cushions of mulch (for the plants and the cat), and beautiful produce

❧ Good for container growing.

❧ Pick off first fruit when it is about 8 cm (3 inches) long. The yield will nearly double with this practice.

❧ Picking crops frequently will also help to increase yield.

Pumpkin

SOIL: Warm, rich, well-drained soil. Give them a lot of space.

SOWING TIME: Sow indoors three to four weeks before last frost. Can also sow directly in garden after risk of frost.

FERTILIZING NEEDS: Feed with 6-12-12 every three weeks.

WATERING NEEDS: Water well when flowers are being produced.

PESTS AND DISEASES: May be attacked by the squash vine borer. See Cucumber entry for symptoms and treatment.

HARVESTING: Cut stem with a sharp knife. The skin of a mature pumpkin cannot be pierced by a fingernail.

COMMENTS:

❧ Susceptible to frost when young.

❧ For bigger pumpkins, and to be sure you'll have a ripe one in time for Halloween, pick off all blossoms after three or four fruits have formed.

Squash

SOIL: Warm, rich, well-drained soil in a sunny, sheltered spot. They sprawl, so you need 3 m (10 feet) of space for the largest ones; half that for smaller ones.

SOWING TIME: To get earlier fruit, start them indoors a couple of weeks before last frost date. Plant seeds or seedlings outside in hills just before last frost date. Protect seedlings on cool nights.

FERTILIZING NEEDS: Feed with 6-12-12 every two weeks.

WATERING NEEDS: Water well during flowering and fruit development and in dry spells.

PESTS AND DISEASES: Susceptible to diseases held in the soil — try to keep water off foliage and prevent soil from splashing on foliage. Don't do any cultivating or harvesting when the plants are wet or damp.

HARVESTING: For summer squash, regular harvesting will keep production up. Young fruits are more flavourful. For winter squash, harvest when vines have died. Skin should be hard enough that it cannot be pierced with a fingernail.

COMMENTS:

- Susceptible to frost.
- Summer squash are good candidates for container growing. A box about 60 cm by 90 cm (2 feet by 3 feet) and 60 cm (2 feet) deep will take one summer squash. Expect its tendrils to tumble down the sides of the box.

Swiss Chard

SOIL: Warm, fertile, moist, well-drained soil.

SOWING TIME: Sow in spring directly in garden one or two weeks before last frost. Also use as succession crop to spinach. Sow in cold frame in midsummer for harvesting in late fall and over the winter. Mulch well.

FERTILIZING NEEDS: If soil is not rich, give a monthly feeding of fish emulsion or similar high-nitrogen fertilizer.

WATERING NEEDS: Keep roots well supplied with moisture all season long or the plant will bolt to seed.

PESTS AND DISEASES: Relatively pest- and disease-free. Pick caterpillars by hand; control aphids with insecticidal soap.

HARVESTING: Cut outer leaves when they are no more than 25 cm (10 inches) long.

COMMENTS:

- Consider planting chard in flower beds, since it is quite ornamental and looks attractive with yellow marigolds and pansies.
- Tolerates heat and frost.

Tomatoes

For many people, nothing says summer better than tomato. Even people who garden in small spaces can often find room for a tomato plant in a container on the balcony or deck or tucked in a sunny corner of the flower bed. Look for early-maturing varieties if you find it hard to wait for that first luscious taste. At the end of the Comments section, I've added a few tips about speeding up the growth of tomatoes — and don't forget the tire trick on page 103 if you live in a place with cool summers.

SOIL: Warm soil in a sheltered spot. Tomatoes love rich, finished compost or composted cattle manure mixed equally with sandy loam.

SOWING TIME: Start seeds indoors six to eight weeks before the last frost. You can transplant seedlings outdoors around the last frost date, but be prepared to institute emergency frost-protection measures. To be safe, wait for a week after the last frost date. Use black plastic to warm the soil. Cut X's into the plastic and plant the tomato in the X. Remove the black plastic before the blossoms set (that is, before fertilization has occurred; the flowers will fade quickly once they've been fertilized).

Getting an Early Tomato Harvest

Here are a few tips for getting an early tomato crop, even if you live in an area where the season is short.

🌱 Look for seeds of varieties that bloom early and set fruit even in fairly cool temperatures. Start the seed indoors early — as early as February in most of Canada. Give seedlings bottom heat, a sunny but cool spot, and moist soil.

🌱 Be prepared to transplant the seedlings to larger containers a couple of times as the plants grow. Trim the longer roots every time you transplant. As well, remove the lower leaves and bring the new soil level up to the top set of leaves so that new roots will form along the buried stem.

🌱 About ten days before the last frost, start hardening off the plants. Set them outside for a longer period every day in a spot where they'll be protected from the wind.

🌱 After ten days of hardening off, transplant them into the garden. Set them in the soil 2.5 to 5 cm (1 to 2 inches) deeper than they were

in their container. Firm the soil around them and water deeply.

🌱 Use some of the season-extending devices I've discussed — cold frames, Wall o' Water, cloches — to give them extra warmth. On frosty nights in particular, protect them well.

The abundant zucchini

FERTILIZING NEEDS: Heavy feeder. Fertilize regularly. Start with a 10-52-10 fertilizer every week for the first three weeks after transplanting, then switch to a small amount of 20-20-20 fertilizer once a week for the rest of the season.

WATERING NEEDS: Water well at least twice a week, especially during flower and fruit development, and every day if weather is hot and dry.

PESTS AND DISEASES: Blossom end rot is thought to be caused by calcium deficiency or very dry weather. You'll know your tomatoes have it if a dark scabby patch appears at the base, or blossom end, of the fruit. Add calcium to the soil by sprinkling crushed eggshells. Tomato horn worms can be hand-picked and destroyed, or apply *Bacillus thuringiensis*. Early blight is a fungus disease that causes spots on foliage and wilting. Prevent by looking for resistant varieties and providing good air circulation.

HARVESTING: I'm tempted to tell you to pick tomatoes when the sight of them makes your mouth water! But if you need guidelines, look for fruits that are slightly soft, completely red, and have a faint fragrance.

COMMENTS:

- Susceptible to frost.
- Some varieties are good for container growing, especially early varieties and cherry tomatoes.
- Determinate plants are bush plants, set all their fruit in a short period of time, do not need pruning, and grow well in cages.
- Indeterminate plants grow tall, produce fruit over the growing season, need pruning, and should be staked.
- Prune indeterminate varieties by pinching out the suckers that grow between the main stem and the branch. This will direct more nutrients and energy to the fruit.
- If you're buying tomato seedlings, look for dark green leaves and a short, stocky stem.
- To get tomatoes to ripen on the vine late in the season, remove all flowers and small tomatoes, leaving only the large fruit; move container-grown plants into a sunnier area; for indeterminate varieties, remove the top set of leaves, thereby directing more energy to the ripening fruit.
- Newspapers or ground-up bark make excellent mulches for tomatoes.
- In late summer, give tomatoes a boost to help them ripen. Dissolve 10 mL (2 tablespoons) Epsom salts in 4.5 L (1 gallon) of water and pour 500 mL (1 pint) around each plant. The magnesium is what does the trick.

Zucchini

SOIL: Warm, rich, well-drained soil in a sunny, protected spot.

SOWING TIME: Sow seeds or transplant seedlings a week after last frost date.

FERTILIZING NEEDS: Feed with 6-12-12 every three weeks.

WATERING NEEDS: Water well once a week in dry spells.

PESTS AND DISEASES: To avoid transmitting diseases, try not to splash soil onto the leaves.

HARVESTING: Pick frequently to keep production going (lack of production is not usually a problem with this vegetable, however!).

COMMENTS:

- Zucchini taste best if harvested when they're young and tender.

Hot-Weather Crops

These crops not only need to be planted after the last frost date, they need continuous heat to produce. Even in the warmest parts of Canada, some of these can be a challenge to grow.

Eggplant

SOIL: Hot soil in a sheltered spot. Will drop flowers and not make new ones if soil is not warm enough. Do not plant where eggplants or strawberries were the previous year.

SOWING TIME: Start seed indoors about ten weeks before last frost. Set out as plants about two weeks after last frost. Be prepared to use cloches at night.

FERTILIZING NEEDS: Medium to heavy feeder

WATERING NEEDS: Water regularly throughout growing season, as eggplants like lots of moisture.

PESTS AND DISEASES: Colorado potato beetles and flea beetles can attack eggplants. Hand-pick them off or spray with rotenone or pyrethrum. Foil cutworms by using paper collars 4 cm (1 1/2 inches) above and below the soil. Try planting garlic and marigolds nearby as repellents.

HARVESTING: Harvesting regularly increases production. Using a sharp knife, pick eggplants when the skin is glossy and fruit is a good size. Wear gloves to protect your hands from their nasty thorns.

Hot-weather crops such as these peppers benefit from protection from cool winds.

COMMENTS:

🌱 Good for container growing.

🌱 Can be a challenge to grow where summers are not long and hot. Look for varieties that mature quickly.

🌱 Stake to keep the fruit off the ground.

🌱 Roots are shallow, so cultivate the soil around the plants carefully. Better yet, mulch so you don't have to cultivate.

Peppers

SOIL: Hot, sandy soil.

SOWING TIME: Sow seeds indoors ten weeks before last frost. Plant out in a sunny sheltered spot when soil and nights are warm.

FERTILIZING NEEDS: Feed with 6-12-12 monthly.

WATERING NEEDS: Water as often as every day if weather is hot and dry.

PESTS AND DISEASES: Colorado potato beetles, flea beetles, and cutworms can be problems. Follow directions for eggplants.

HARVESTING: Picking frequently will encourage more fruiting.

COMMENTS:

🌱 Good for container growing.

🌱 Peppers do not like cold weather. Bring plants indoors in the fall and place in a sunny location. Be sure to spray with an insecticidal soap so you don't also bring in insects. Peppers should keep producing until the end of the year.

🌱 Dry peppers by stringing them like a necklace and hanging them in a cool, well-ventilated room.

Permanent Crops

Even gardeners who don't grow food crops often have a rhubarb plant tucked away in a corner. And who hasn't dreamed of picking fresh asparagus and strawberries from one's own plants? If you've inherited any of these and they seem healthy and productive, it may be because the bed was well prepared. If you're adding any of them to your garden, it will be worth your time to do the same careful preparations — after all, it's harder to amend the soil once these permanent crops are in place.

Asparagus is an extremely hardy and reliable performer for years on end, as is that old-fashioned favourite, rhubarb. Both are easy-care plants. Strawberries demand a bit more space and attention. The results, though, are worth it!

Asparagus

SOIL: Well-cultivated, well-drained soil in full sun; not partial to acid soil.

SOWING TIME: Plant crowns in early spring. (Growing from seed delays first harvest for three or four years. Two-year-old crowns are available from most garden centres.)

FERTILIZING NEEDS: Once a week for the first three weeks, fertilize new plants with 10-52-10 to establish a good root system. Likes composted manure and phosphorus (bone meal). Feed once a month from May to July with 6-12-12.

WATERING NEEDS: Water after the harvest is over and give a final good watering in October.

PESTS AND DISEASES: Pest- and disease-resistant, except for the asparagus beetle. Signs are young shoots that have been chewed; the spears will be distorted as they grow and leaves will be damaged. The small beetle is blue-black and has red and black spots. Treat with lime or rotenone. Asparagus sometimes falls prey to rust, which can be avoided by planting rust-resistant varieties such as 'Martha Washington,' or spraying with garden sulphur.

HARVESTING: Harvest in spring when spears show through the soil, but do not harvest first year you plant; harvest sparingly next year. Use a sharp knife to cut the spears or snap them off just below soil level.

COMMENTS:

- When preparing a new bed for asparagus, be meticulous about clearing out all perennial weeds, and be especially careful to eradicate twitch, or couch, grass. Turn the soil and add well-rotted manure and compost.
- Add manure and a mulch over the bed every year.
- To get white spears, mound the soil over the shoots as they grow.
- Leave at least one-third of the crop to grow into ferns—don't prune them, because they will help to trap the snow, providing insulation and moisture for the roots.
- Keep bed well weeded to avoid attracting insects and to retain all nutrients for the plants.
- This is one of those plants that need a dormant period in the winter; it does not survive in warm climates.

Make room for a row of asparagus — you'll never regret it.

Rhubarb

SOIL: Well-drained, rich soil.

SOWING TIME: Plant roots in early spring or late fall.

FERTILIZING NEEDS: Heavy feeder. Add well-rotted manure or compost and use organic mulch every year.

WATERING NEEDS: Requires no special attention.

PESTS AND DISEASES: Slugs are really the only pest that attacks rhubarb.

HARVESTING: Don't harvest in the first year, and in the second take only the largest stalks for about two weeks.

COMMENTS:

* Rhubarb is red-stalked ('Canada Red,' 'Crimson Red,' 'Valentine') or green-stalked ('Sutton's,' 'Victoria').

Strawberries

SOIL: Well-drained, light soil with lots of organic matter worked in.

SOWING TIME: Plant in spring.

FERTILIZING NEEDS: Fertilize at planting time. Mulch with straw, hay, or plastic.

WATERING NEEDS: Water well during flowering and when runners are being produced.

PESTS AND DISEASES: Slugs, as well as birds, can attack strawberries.

HARVESTING: Strawberries are ready for picking a month after blooming. Don't allow blossoms to form the first year (see Comments section).

COMMENTS:

* When planting strawberries, set the plant into the soil to where the leaves and roots meet (the crown).

Rhubarb: another spring treat

- Pinch out all first-season buds. On ever-bearing plants, pinch until the end of June for a small harvest the first year.
- For good yields in subsequent years, cut off runners (new shoots), but leave some runners to root to provide new plants.
- To protect plants over the winter, cover with straw or evergreen branches.

Crop Rotation

Why is it important to rotate most vegetable crops every year or so? Replanting in the same soil often means a plant is even more vulnerable to the diseases and insects that the family is generally susceptible to. If you plant potatoes in the same soil three years in a row, I guarantee that Colorado potato beetles will invade in short order in most parts of Canada.

Rotating your crops in the vegetable garden and cold frame generally leads to healthier plants. By both rotating crops and adding compost or other humusy material to your vegetable beds every year, you'll have extremely healthy soil.

Different plant families have different nutritional requirements, so it's better to put a crop that's a light feeder, such as beets or onions, in a place where heavy feeders, such as potatoes or tomatoes, grew the year before.

Here's some information to help you plan your crop rotation.
- Vegetables that are light feeders are beets, carrots, garlic, onions, parsnips, and radishes.
- Vegetables that are medium feeders are beans, broccoli, Brussels sprouts, eggplant, kale, kohlrabi, leeks, lettuce, peas, peppers, rutabaga, spinach, Swiss chard, turnips, zucchini.
- Vegetables that are heavy feeders are asparagus, cabbage, cauliflower, celeriac, celery, corn, cucumbers, melons, potatoes, pumpkins, squash, tomatoes.

Succession Planting

You might be doing succession planting without even being aware of it. The term can refer to sowing successive plantings of, say, lettuce, or choosing varieties of lettuce that have different maturity dates so that you have a continual supply for as long as possible. It can also refer to the practice of replacing harvested crops with different crops appropriate to the growing season. If you've been practising succession planting on a haphazard basis, do some planning this year so you can use your garden space more intensively.
- Plan to use early, middle, and late varieties, which will all be planted at the same time but will mature at different dates, spreading your harvest of that crop over a longer period.
- Start a second group of seeds indoors or in the cold frame, to be ready for transplanting as various crops are harvested. Crops that lend themselves to a second planting or a first planting to succeed other harvested crops are cabbage, cauliflower, broccoli, Brussels sprouts, endive, escarole, and collard greens.
- Sow seeds of the same variety every week or so, as long as the conditions that the plant needs in order to germinate and grow are still present.

Folk Wisdom

Plant your corn when oak leaves are as big as a mouse's ear.

When lilacs begin to leaf out, plant peas, lettuce, and spinach. When lilacs are in full bloom, plant corn, tomatoes, and basil.

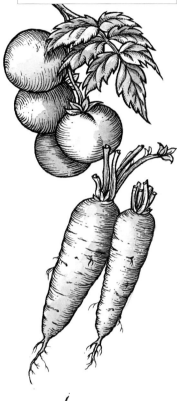

Rule of Thumb

Try planting chrysanthemums, marigolds, or chives around your vegetable garden. I've found they will repel insects.

Companion Planting

Not everyone believes that companion planting works. It's based mainly on folklore and individual observation, rather than scientifically proven tests. The reputed benefits include repelling pests and enhancing growth. You're unlikely to harm any crops by trying it, and it might have beneficial results.

Companion planting probably isn't quite the correct term for those plants that *don't* like to be planted near one another, but I'm including them in the list. Growing these foes together can cause one to curtail the growth of the other or produce stunted growth, so avoid the unfriendly combinations I've noted.

Asparagus: Plant near basil, parsley, and tomatoes. Don't grow near onions.

Basil: Plant with tomatoes and asparagus.

Beans: Plant near corn, squash, and members of the cabbage family. They fix nitrogen in the soil. Marigolds planted near beans help repel Mexican bean beetles. Don't plant with beets.

Beets: Plant near members of the cabbage family, leafy greens, garlic, and onions. Don't plant with beans.

Borage: Grows well near tomatoes and spinach. Also attracts bees, which assist in pollination of all plants.

Broccoli: Plant near herbs: dill, mint, rosemary, camomile, and sage. Likes beets, cucumbers, lettuce, onions, radishes, potatoes, marigolds, and nasturtiums.

Brussels sprouts: Same as for broccoli.

Cabbage: Same as for broccoli.

Carrots: Grow near tomatoes, cucumbers, beans, chives, onions, lettuce, radishes, peas, and sage. Don't grow near dill.

Cauliflower: Same as for broccoli.

Chervil: Plant near radishes. The flowers are host to beneficial insects.

Chives: Plant near carrots, tomatoes, and lettuce, and not near peas and beans.

Cucumbers: Plant near radishes, beans, broccoli, Brussels sprouts, cabbage, cauliflower, peas, tomatoes, marigolds, nasturtiums, oregano. Don't grow near sage.

Dill: Plant near broccoli, Brussels sprouts, cabbage, cauliflower, onions, and lettuce. Don't plant near carrots or tomatoes. The flowers are host to beneficial insects, especially the monarch butterfly larvae.

Eggplant: Plant near beans, tarragon, thyme, and marigolds.

Fennel: Plant near thyme and sage. The flowers are host to beneficial insects. Don't plant near coriander, bush beans, or tomatoes.

Garlic: Plant anywhere to repel many different insects.

Lettuce: Plant near cabbage, beets, carrots, chives, garlic, and onions. Don't plant near broccoli.

Nasturtiums: Use to attract aphids away from other plants. Also repel other insects. Plant with beans, peppers, broccoli, Brussels sprouts, cabbage, and cauliflower.

Onions: Plant near beets, carrots, lettuce, potatoes, broccoli, Brussels sprouts, cabbage, and cauliflower. Don't plant near sage and peas.

Parsley: Plant near asparagus, corn, and tomatoes.

Peas: Plant near tomatoes, eggplant, lettuce, spinach, peppers, corn, radishes, cucumbers, carrots, and beans.

Peppers: Plant near carrots, onions, marigolds, basil, marjoram, or oregano. Don't plant near eggplant, tomatoes, or fennel.

Radishes: Plant near beans, lettuce, cabbage, or tomatoes, chervil, peas, parsnips, onions, carrots, cucumbers, and squash.

Sage: Plant near cabbage, carrots, tomatoes, or marjoram. The flowers attract bees. Don't plant near cucumbers.

Spinach: Plant near borage, eggplant, broccoli, Brussels sprouts, cabbage, cauliflower, peas, onions, marigolds, nasturtiums, beans, and oregano. Don't plant near potatoes.

Squash: Plant near beans, corn, sunflowers, marigolds, nasturtiums, radishes, and mints. Don't plant near potatoes.

Thyme: Plant near asparagus, cabbage, carrots, cucumbers, onions, peppers, marigolds, bee balm, basil, borage, parsley, and sage. Don't plant near corn, dill, and potatoes.

Revisiting the Cold Frame

Many of the seedlings that you moved to the cold frame for hardening off are ready for setting out into the garden. Unfortunately, the date for doing this can't be generalized — it will differ from zone to zone and from year to year. The conflict between the desire to continue nurturing the plants in the cold frame (and possibly watching them become leggy) and the fear that a killing frost will get them is a hard one to resolve. The best advice I can give you is to listen to the weather forecast and choose a time when the temperatures are mild, there's cloud cover, and some rain is predicted. These provide the ideal conditions for moving the seedlings. If the weather is unrelentingly sunny, do your transplanting late in the day.

Transplant the cool-weather seedlings first, and be prepared to protect them if frost threatens; don't forget to remove the protection during the day.

Water the seedlings to be transplanted and take them to the bed in small batches. For each seedling, make a small hole — about twice the size of the root ball — and stir in a bit of sifted compost. Carefully remove the seedling from its container and place it in the prepared hole so that it's planted just a bit deeper than it was before. Pat the soil gently around the plant, creating a small depression around the plant to catch water. Water the seedlings, adding some fish emulsion to make a weak fertilizer mixture if you desire. If the subsequent days are hot and dry or windy, shade the seedlings with boxes, paper bags, or floating row covers.

As space in the cold frame is freed up through transplanting the cool-weather crops, any warm-weather and hot-weather seedlings still indoors can be moved to the cold frame, and the same process of hardening off prior to transplanting followed.

Rule of Thumb
Practise good garden hygiene in the cold frame by immediately getting rid of all damaged or sick-looking plants or vegetation.

Kids' Gardening:
Growing Everlastings for Dried Flower Arrangements

Children seem to be attracted to the unusual in the plant world, and many plants that can be used for everlasting dried flower arrangements are unusual and easy to grow, making them perfect for the kids' garden. Here are some annual plants that work well in dried arrangements. Plant in full sun unless otherwise specified. None of them need special care in drying; just hang upside down in loosely tied bunches in an airy, dry place.

Bells of Ireland (*Molucella laevis*): Cup-shaped green bracts grow along the 60 to 90 cm (2- to 3-foot) stem, giving this plant its name. As the plant grows, it may be necessary to stake it. Pick when fully developed and hang to dry. The bracts keep their shape and become a lovely ivory-gold colour.

Chinese Lanterns (*Physalis*): Children love the delightful orange lanterns of this plant, which grows to about 45 cm (18 inches). Cut just as they start to colour and hang to dry.

Money Plant (*Lunaria*): The coinlike white seed pods are the attraction here; they form after the rather in-significant white blooms have finished. Be warned that the money plant self-

seeds and you will have seedlings popping up for many years.

Rose Everlasting (*Helipterum roseum*): The flower is pink and dai-sylike and the plant grows to about 45 cm (1½ feet) in height. Cut just before the flowers open, strip off leaves, and hang to dry.

Statice (*Limonium*): Statice, with its papery flowers, comes in a satisfying array of colours: yellow, white, pink, lavender, and blue. Pick when about two-thirds of the flowers have opened, and hang to dry.

Strawflowers (*Helichrysumi*): One of the easiest everlastings to grow, strawflowers can get as tall as 1.2 m (4 feet). Their many-petalled flowers come in yellow, red, white, and blue. Pick just before the flower opens.

Drying Tips
* A dry, dark, ventilated room is the best place to dry flowers.
* Harvest flowers or foliage at mid-day when the plants are dry. Avoid cutting after heavy rain or dew.
* When preparing for drying, strip the leaves off the stems and tie stems together in small bunches with string or elastic ties.

LEFT, TOP TO BOTTOM:
Strawflowers, statice, and money plant
TOP RIGHT:
Three dried rose bouquets. These will prove more challenging but can be tried once the basics of drying are understood.

May Gardening Checklist

General

🌱 Take out hoses and inspect for leaks. Start watering lawns and beds if necessary. Keep seedlings watered.

Ornamental Garden

🌱 Plant out purchased bedding plants after middle of month, keeping in mind your last frost date.

🌱 Pinch chrysanthemums and asters to encourage bushy growth (see Chapter 6).

🌱 Prune candles of compact conifers.

Zones 2 to 6

🌱 Early in month, start to remove winter mulches from perennials gradually; add new mulches when ground is warm.

🌱 Remove faded flower heads from tulips and daffodils, being sure to leave stem and foliage.

🌱 Start to keep weeds under control. Cultivate or hoe all exposed soils — better yet, mulch if ground has warmed up.

🌱 Check trees for tent caterpillars. Break any tents you find.

🌱 Harden off and plant out annual seedlings.

🌱 Sow seeds outdoors for hardy annual flowers.

🌱 Prune evergreen shrubs and hedges for shape.

🌱 Prune roses when frost danger has passed.

🌱 Prune early-flowering shrubs after bloom is done.

🌱 Plant summer bulbs (see Chapter 8).

Zones 7 to 9

🌱 Mulch roses if not done already.

🌱 Prune shrubs that have finished flowering.

🌱 Plant dahlia tubers.

Fruit and Vegetable Garden

Zones 2 to 6

🌱 Plant strawberries and raspberries.

🌱 Harden off and transplant broccoli, pepper, and tomato seedlings.

🌱 Use season-extending devices to protect young seedlings.

Zones 7 to 9

🌱 Continue with successive sowings of lettuce, carrots, spinach, radishes, beans, and potatoes.

🌱 Sow cauliflower, broccoli, Brussels sprouts, cabbages, and pumpkins. Sow corn and cucumber at end of month.

🌱 Plant out seedlings of tomatoes, peppers, eggplants, zucchini, and squash.

Chapter 6

June

A Month of Joy

In many regions, June is the month gardeners take the most pride in their gardens. Roses are bursting into a riot of colours, silken poppies glimmer in the sun, the tiny seeds sown so hopefully in the cool spring are now lush plants threatening to take over the bed. Of course you want this beauty and this bounteous harvest to continue. To keep your plants attractive and producing well, use the following techniques throughout the summer months.

Mulching

Mulching is the practice of adding a protective layer of organic or inorganic material on top of soil around plants or over plants. Mulching plants, whether ornamental or food-producing, is done for many reasons:

- It keeps weeds down.
- It conserves moisture.
- It nourishes the soil (true only of organic mulches).
- It insulates the soil and regulates its temperature.
- It protects plants from the freeze-thaw-freeze cycle.
- It helps loosen compacted soil, especially clay soils (true only of organic mulches, which break down to add a layer of fluffier material).
- It prevents erosion and the leaching-out of nutrients.
- It protects plants from being splashed by raindrops, not only making them more attractive but avoiding the soil-borne diseases splashing can transmit.
- It protects the fruits of sprawling plants from dirt.
- It can extend the gardening season by a couple of weeks.
- It helps newly pruned plants recover from the shock of pruning.
- It frees up the gardener for other gardening tasks or just for enjoying the garden because there's less weeding and watering to do!

I must admit I was a slow convert to mulching until a friend showed me how much soil he lost every year to wind erosion on his fields. Now it's a regular part of my gardening practices.

Because mulch has an insulating effect, you have to be aware of how it works at different seasons of the year and use it accordingly.

In the summer, mulch is applied only to the ground around plants — it should not touch them — and is used primarily to keep weeds under control and to conserve

It's not hard to make the June garden lush. Poppies gleam and shimmer in the summer sun (ABOVE); azaleas flourish in partial shade, their roots protected with mulch.

moisture. Spring mulching will prevent the soil from warming and will cause severe retardation in germination, so don't add mulch until seedlings are well established and perennials are robust. Once transplants are firmly established or seeds are sprouting nicely (about 2.5 cm/1 inch tall), you can start adding mulch for the reasons given earlier — keeping down weeds and conserving moisture, for example. Crops that like cooler weather flourish when they're mulched — beets, carrots, peas, lettuce, cabbage, broccoli, Brussels sprouts, potatoes, cauliflower, spinach, radishes, and turnips. Mulch should *never* touch the trunk or stem of anything newly planted or the stem could rot.

If your summers are cool, short, or damp, mulching may not be appropriate. If you decide you want to mulch anyway, don't mulch heat-loving crops — such as tomatoes, peppers, melons, grapes, eggplant, squash, and pumpkins — early in the season. They need all the warmth they can get in order to prosper.

Mulching Materials

Most mulching materials are organic, and thus break down slowly, releasing nutrients to the soil over time. They improve soil texture and tilth, making it looser and more friable, and improve conditions for micro-organisms and earthworms, which help to "mix" the soil up. Inorganic mulches such as plastic don't break down, but they do warm the soil up quickly, and are extremely efficient at keeping weeds down and conserving moisture. Some inorganic mulches, especially plastic, don't allow air and moisture through; and using them for a whole season can have a damaging effect on your garden.

Mulching material: peat moss (TOP LEFT), *cocoa shells* (TOP RIGHT), *sawdust* (BOTTOM LEFT), *redwood bark chips* (BOTTOM RIGHT)

The following are some materials that are suitable for mulching. I've designated some as cooling mulch — those that cool the soil — to help you plan your use of mulches wisely. Anything not described as nonbiodegradable will decompose.

Aluminized paper (nonbiodegradable): Available from garden centres, this cooling mulch suppresses weeds well. Extend at least 15 cm (6 inches) out from plant; lay in single sheets, weight edges with soil, cut X-shaped slits for seeds or seedlings.

Bark chips: Don't break down easily, and because of their attractive colour and texture are used for decorative purposes mainly.

Black plastic (nonbiodegradable): Good for warming soil and keeping weeds down. Fertilize and water soil, lay down plastic, weight edges with soil or rocks, slit plastic where you want the plant, pop in the seedling. Use for heat-loving vegetables such as tomatoes, peppers, cucumbers, squash, corn, eggplant. Can also be applied in strips on either side of plantings. The plastic generally lasts only one season.

Buckwheat hulls: Good for roses, perennials, and tuberous begonias.

Clear plastic (nonbiodegradable): Good for use in the north; can provide an early start, since it warms soil better than black plastic, but weeds will grow under it (in very hot weather, however, weeds under clear plastic will be killed by the excessive heat); don't use for shrubs, trees, or ornamental gardens.

Cocoa shells: Break down quickly (and they do have a chocolatey aroma!).

Compost: One of the best all-purpose mulches; improves soil texture and fertilizes; you can use partially decomposed compost for mulch.

Corncobs, ground: Good for roses; reputed to rob plants of nitrogen.

Evergreen branches: Use branches stripped from a discarded Christmas tree as a light winter mulch over perennials, also to protect heathers, azaleas, and rhododendrons from burning in winter sun.

Mulching young plants in the vegetable garden is especially important to help conserve moisture and make it available to the tender roots.

ABOVE LEFT:
More mulching material: stones (TOP LEFT), *leaf mould* (TOP RIGHT), *shredded newspaper* (BOTTOM LEFT), *fine bark* (BOTTOM RIGHT)

Plastic mulches

Grass clippings: Cooling mulch that improves texture. For flower or vegetable beds, let dry before using, and don't use more than 2.5 cm (1 inch) of clippings. Don't use clippings from grass that has been sprayed with herbicide — it can harm plants.

Hay: Cooling mulch; best kind is spoiled hay, which has already begun to decompose; fresh hay may contain many weed seeds.

Landscape fabrics (nonbiodegradable): Synthetic fabrics made of polyester, nylon, or polypropylene; air and water can pass through them; last several seasons; use as you do plastic; you can cover with a more attractive organic mulch such as bark or cocoa shells.

Leaf mould: Leaves that are partially decayed; can be used everywhere in the garden as a rich mulch.

Leaves: Break down very slowly, sometimes mat, cutting off air and water from the roots; should be put through shredder, run over with lawn mower, or composted before being used as mulch; dried leaves can be used as a light winter mulch over perennials, but in a rainy winter, remove them if they seem to be matted.

Manure: Fresh manure will burn, so use well-rotted manure.

Newspaper: Cooling mulch; apply either layered or shredded; don't use anything with shiny stock or coloured inks; needs to be anchored; try wetting it first, to stop it blowing around; when used in excess — more than 6 mm (1/4 inch) or eight to ten pages — it can rob soil of nitrogen.

Peat moss: Best used mixed with sawdust, wood chips, or soil, as it tends to dry out and form a crust that water cannot penetrate; always dampen it first; provides no nutrition to plants, but is a good mulch for acid-loving plants.

Pebbles and stones: Suppress weeds well; good for use around trees, shrubs, and in rock gardens; hold warmth from the day and release it gradually at night.

Pine needles: Improve soil texture; provide acidity; can take nitrogen out of the soil as they decompose; control fungal diseases to a degree.

Salt hay: Good for sandy soil and fruit trees; can rob soil of nitrogen.

Sawdust: Provides acidity; can rob soil of nitrogen as it decomposes, so it's best to use a high-nitrogen fertilizer first or, ideally, let it age for a year before using; good for vegetables and blueberries.

Seaweed: Adds potassium and trace elements as it decomposes; if you collect your own, wash it well to remove the salt before using or leave it exposed to the elements for a few months; also reputed to repel slugs and snails; not particularly attractive.

Straw: Cooling mulch; builds tilth; some urban garden centres carry bales in the autumn; good for sandy soil and fruit trees, potatoes, and strawberries; shouldn't contain weed seeds, but often does.

Wood chips: Provide acidity; can take nitrogen out of the soil as they decompose, so best not used on vegetable garden.

Mulching Vegetables

Researchers in Connecticut have experimented to see what happens when mulches are used in combination with one another in the vegetable garden. Their best yields (not necessarily their earliest) came from peppers grown in soil covered with a triple-layer mulch of clear plastic over black plastic over leaves. They found that warming mulches encouraged blossom-end rot in crops such as tomatoes and peppers if the mulches were left on after fruit set. With such crops, mulch when transplanted, but remove when the first few fruits have set. After about a week, replace the mulch with a cool one, such as grass clippings, straw, or hay.

These studies also found that it is best to mulch only once the soil temperature reaches 25°C (78°F) 8 to 10 cm (3 to 4 inches) below the surface. You might not want to get this scientific, but armed with this knowledge about mulches, you can begin to do your own experimenting. For example, you might start to group your vegetables by their season length and their liking for warm or cool soil, and mulch accordingly. At the end of the season, use plastic strips to keep the soil warm for crops with longer seasons.

Herb gardens benefit from rock or pebble mulches. (You can warm up beds in the spring by setting large flat stones over the surface of a bed and around the edges; remove the stones when the soil has warmed up.) Many herbs grow naturally in rocky, dry soil, and herbs, such as parsley, are healthier grown among pebbles or rocks.

A well-mulched vegetable garden

Rule of Thumb

In very dry weather, soak the soil before mulching it.

Make sure all perennial weeds are removed before mulching — otherwise they'll benefit just as much as your plants.

Slugs and Mulches

It's true that slugs like mulches — for them, it's a nice cool, dark place to get out of the summer sun. Don't let that deter you from using mulches. Slugs prefer an air temperature between 15°C and 21°C (60 and 70°F). That's when they're most active. Temperatures above 27°C (80°F) make them. . . well, sluggish. If you have slug problems, put off using mulch until the days are hotter, and take it off before the temperatures return to the slugs' preferred range in the fall.

Mulching Fruit Trees

Mulch has the same moderating influence on the soil around fruit trees as it does on the soil in the rest of the garden. This is one case where you should consider mulching early in the spring, for the very reason that it slows down growth and blooming. In our unpredictable climate, it's not unusual for spring to appear suddenly, causing fruit trees to bloom early, then for freezing weather to reappear quickly, damaging the blossoms and leading to a reduced harvest. It's much safer to try to delay the blooms by mulching in early spring, thereby keeping the soil cool.

Make sure the mulch extends well out from the tree — the spread of the mulch should equal the spread of the crown of the tree.

Encouraging Summer Blooms

As I mentioned earlier, there are a number of techniques you can use to keep plants blooming for longer periods. Most of these techniques work on the "cutting back" principle: that is, you thwart the plant's growth in the short term so it puts a lot of energy into bigger and better blooms.

Deadheading: Deadheading, contrary to its rather gruesome-sounding name, encourages plants to continue blooming. The term refers to the removal of fading and spent flowers on annuals and perennials. This prevents plants from going to seed, forcing them to put forth more blooms, and can stop them from becoming too leggy. On some flowers, such as daisies, deadheading can involve taking part of the stem, as well, cutting just above new flower buds.

Keep the garden tidy by cutting back spent blooms of perennials; you might even be rewarded with another period of bloom.

Don't deadhead chives if you want to use the flowers as colourful accents in your garden — or cut them to scatter in a summer salad.

For some plants, deadhead timing is very important. I remove the spent blooms from my rhododendrons every year, but only when they snap off with a simple twist so that the clean break does not damage the tiny new growth bud at the base of the dead flower stalk.

Pinching: Pinching is performed to make a plant grow bushy and more compact. Pinching will delay flowering and the flowers will be smaller than an unpinched plant's, but they will be more numerous. To pinch back a plant, just remove its growing tips, the part that is usually just above the uppermost set of leaves. Plants such as asters and chrysanthemums that flower in the late summer and autumn respond well to pinching.

Stems can get leggy on annuals such as petunias, geraniums, browallia, lobelia, and ivies. Keep them bushy and blooming by pinching back stems just above a set of leaves. Within a couple of weeks, new side branching and flowers will form.

Disbudding: As you might guess, this practice removes the buds from a plant. The removal of side buds causes the terminal bud to produce one large flower on a long stem. If the terminal bud is removed, the side buds will produce many small flowers. The practice is used most often on flowers grown for showing.

Cutting back: Some gardeners are just as fearful of cutting back as they are of a full-fledged pruning, but the benefits are worth the trauma (both the gardener's and the plant's!). Over the course of a season, some plants, especially herbs, will begin to get leggy and scrawny-looking. Take pity on the poor plant and prune it to a nice shape. You'll be rewarded with a burst of healthy new growth and, quite likely, another round of blooms. Some of the taller perennials will take quite a severe cutting back, even down to the new foliage at their base. They will soon put on new growth and perhaps go through another blooming period, although this is likely to be less robust than the first.

Annuals such as sweet alyssum, lobelia, petunias, and annual candytuft sometimes begin to look a bit ragged by the middle of the summer. Cut back their stems by one-third to give them a new lease on life. Asters can be encouraged to bush out more and produce more blooms by cutting back the foliage by about half in June.

I will often use a pair of gardening shears to cut back all my petunias just before taking off on a summer vacation. My neighbours are left with a strange view, but then we all reap the benefits two or three weeks later when the shortened plants burst forth with a new set of blooms to last all summer.

Astilbe

Caring for Your Perennials

Most perennials have a relatively short blooming period — compared with annuals, anyway — so that even the most religious deadheading will not keep them blooming for the entire season. But even when they're not in bloom, they require some care.

❧ In early summer, cut back the perennials that have bloomed in the spring. Snip off dead flower heads and cut back the stems to the ground. In the case of bulbs, don't cut out the yellowing foliage, which helps the bulb store energy and nutrients for the next year; leave the foliage to die down on its own.

❧ For plants with a single stem that carries no leaves, such as red-hot poker, cut back right to the base at ground level when flowering has finished.

❧ For plants that carry leaves on their stems, cut back the stem to just below the top leaves when flowering is done.

❧ Some plants, especially those that grow in rock gardens or that are used as edgings, form mats and often become straggly. After they have finished blooming, use scissors or shears to prune them back hard to about half or two-thirds of their original height. They will put out new growth and may even bloom a second time.

- If the perennial's leaves start to look scraggly, dry, or brown, cut them back to about 5 to 8 cm (2 to 3 inches) from the ground. They'll put out new leaves. It's a good idea not to cut back hard after the middle of July, though, because the plant needs time to recover before getting ready to head into winter.

- Take note of plants that need dividing. Suddenly that showpiece can start starving and crowding out other less invasive or robust treasures. Keep a list or mark the plants in some way — perhaps a small coloured stick or plastic straw stuck into the soil next to the offender — so you are reminded which plants need dividing next fall or spring.

- Stake plants that are getting too tall. Delphiniums probably head the list of plants that need staking, but others could include balloon flower, tall asters, and tall trumpet lilies. Take care not to damage the plant's roots if you are using stakes.

- Water deeply when the soil is dry. Plants can become stressed, too, when it's both sunny and windy. If they're drooping in the late afternoon, it doesn't necessarily mean they need watering — if they perk up in the early evening, they're okay. But if they're drooping in the morning or evening, they're in need of water. Water early in the day so plants can absorb the moisture before the sun begins to dry them out. For more hints about watering, see Chapter 7.

- Keep an eye out for munching pests. Spraying with an insecticidal soap should keep most of them at bay. However, if you're dealing with a severe infestation, you may want to experiment with some of the other methods listed on pages 143 to 151. Slugs seem to be the most common pest problem, followed, these days, by earwigs (they do have a saving grace, though — they prey on other insects, such as aphids and whitefly).

- Keep weeds down, especially in the early part of the season.

Weeding

Weeds are more than just unattractive members of your garden. They are thieves. They steal light, water, and nutrients that should be going to your plants. Mulching, of course, helps to keep weeds under control, but on the East and West Coasts, gardeners who have problems with slugs might prefer not to mulch. As well, before you start to mulch, while you're waiting for the soil to warm up, the weeds will be getting a good start.

Many people moan about weeding, but it can be a pleasant, and even rewarding, experience. In fact, after a hectic day at the garden centre or answering callers' questions on my radio show, I find an hour or so of quietly pulling weeds wonderfully therapeutic. Not only are you doing something useful, but you're getting to know your garden and the plants and animals that live there up close. This is a basic, down-to-the-earth aspect of gardening!

A good first step to eradicating weeds can be taken in the spring, a few weeks before you'll start your planting, when you are preparing your ground. Pull out all grass and weed roots as you dig and rake your beds. Any weed seeds that your cultivation has brought to the top will have a chance to germinate. In a couple of weeks, lightly cultivate the bed again, "stirring" the soil to get rid of those weed seedlings. You can practise stirring the soil after the bed is seeded, since most

Folk Wisdom

One year's seeding means seven years' weeding.

Phlox

vegetable seeds are planted more deeply than the part of the soil you'll be moving around. Let your own plantings be your guide as to when you try stirring, a time-honoured, weed-prevention method. Once your crops are sprouting into seedlings, continue this gentle cultivation between the rows and weeding will not be tedious. When I worked on our nursery farm as a teenager, my father used to remind me daily, "If you just *move* those weeds as tiny seedlings, hoeing will never seem like a chore."

Keep lawns and areas around vegetable and fruit beds mowed so weeds don't get the chance to go to seed and blow into your garden. It's important to get to them before they go to seed for two reasons: you don't want to be tossing weed seeds on the compost pile, and you don't want weed seeds scattering themselves all over the garden.

In the vegetable garden, as crops are harvested, put in a new planting of fall vegetables or cover crop so that the ground is not lying unused, an open invitation to weeds. In the ornamental garden, pop in annuals or mulch in spots where perennials have not yet spread sufficiently to prevent weeds from sprouting.

When you weed, it's important to get rid of all of the plant—roots and seeds or flowers, as well. Merely cutting weeds down will have the same effect as pruning your other plants—they will come back with vigour.

If weeds have become fairly tall, pull them shortly after a rain or a thorough watering. They'll come out of the earth more easily.

Annual and Perennial Weeds

Just as there are annual and perennial flowers, so there are annual and perennial weeds. Both types of weed are difficult to eradicate—annuals because they spread their seeds widely, perennials because they often have deep taproots.

Annual weeds: Keep beds well covered with mulch to prevent the seeds from germinating. Hoe emerging weed seedlings as soon as they sprout.

Perennial weeds: Dig up as many roots or rhizomes as possible. Although this can be difficult, remember to get every bit.

As a last resort, use chemical weed killers. Choose the one for your particular problem and follow the directions to the letter. You are handling poisons when you use weed killers.

Do weeds have any benefits? Well, a few. They bring nutrients from deeper in the soil closer to the surface; they can contribute to compost; their deep roots help to break up heavy soil; their flowers attract butterflies and hummingbirds just as successfully as cultivated flowers do; and they can sometimes signal the type of soil you've got.

* Clover, vetch, and members of the pea family indicate a soil that is low in nitrogen.
* Nettle grows in a rich soil that is high in phosphorus.
* When chicory is blue, it indicates soil with a high lime content; when chicory is pink, the soil is very acidic.
* Goldenrod and bindweed generally grow in sandy soils.
* Sedge signals that the soil is salty.

Dealing with Pests

To get the best from your garden, whether it's your ornamental border or the vegetable bed, you want your plants to be healthy. Healthy plants will give larger, better blooms, fruits, and vegetables and will better withstand stresses over which you have little control—wind and cold, for example.

Ensuring you have healthy plants means keeping your garden clean of plant debris, which can harbour pests and diseases; maintaining the health of your soil; supplying the plants with adequate nutrients and water; planting varieties that are resistant to disease and pests that might strike in your area; practising crop rotation; and checking for insect pests and getting rid of them.

On the rounds of your garden, look out for pest warning signs, such as chewed leaves, ragged leaf edges, leaves that are rolled up, and holes in leaves and flower buds. Check for culprits on the underside of leaves and petals and at the juncture of stems and branches. For example, aphids and the eggs of the Colorado potato

> **Rule of Thumb**
> Composted or dried manure is preferable to fresh manure for many reasons, one of which is that it contains fewer weed seeds.

Aloe vera produces a gel that can be used to repel insects.

beetle are often found on the underside of leaves; mealybugs appear on stems. Gently shaking a plant will reveal if whiteflies are present — they will fly up in a little cloud.

Here are some general ideas for insect control. Also check out the rogues' gallery of unwelcome insects in the next few pages for specific suggestions.

- Simply pick off or cut off the offending part of the plant. If you see a rolled-up leaf, chances are there's a small worm or caterpillar inside. Just snip the leaf off, worm and all. I step on it, but you can also collect them in a bag that you put in the garbage — not in the compost.

- The aloe vera plant contains a bitter-tasting gel that insects don't like. Mix the gel with water and spray it on plants.

- Try dislodging the pests with a hard spray of water from a hose. This works especially well with spider mites.

- Attract birds to your garden by putting out water and seed for them in the summer. They will reward you by eating many insects.

Most gardeners today know the dangers of chemical insecticides. Not only can these chemicals be damaging to humans and the environment in general, they can be damaging to the beneficial insects (described later in this chapter) that you want to encourage. Many manufacturers are providing us with safe alternatives to the poisons we used in the past for dealing with insect infestations; also, there are many tried-and-true home mixtures you can make yourself. The following list describes some safer alternatives and home remedies.

Bacillus thuringiensis (B.t.): A parasitic bacteria sold in spray form, which controls such insects as cabbageworms, tomato hornworms, tent caterpillars, and gypsy moths. It is effective only when the insect is at the caterpillar stage.

Diatomaceous earth: A nontoxic powder made of the pulverized remains of fossilized sea creatures, it causes many insects to dry up and die. Although it's safe to warm-blooded animals, it kills most insects, good and bad. Use with caution and always wear a dust mask when applying.

Homemade Pest Control

Make Your Own Insecticidal Soap

Mix 30 mL (2 tablespoons) of biodegradable soap (a pure soap like Ivory is good) with 1 L (1 quart) of water. Stir thoroughly and use in a plant sprayer.

Make Your Own Sticky Strips

Spread honey, maple syrup, or a similar sticky substance on yellow paper or plastic. Hang near plants when the flies of damaging insects become evident.

Beneficial insects are attracted to these traps, too, so take down as soon as the infestation seems to have cleared up.

Apply a sticky substance to an apple to attract and trap insects (LEFT); Tree Tanglefoot applied to birch trees (ABOVE).

Dormant oil spray: A commercially available mineral oil applied in a thin layer to dormant fruit trees and ornamental trees and shrubs; usually combined with lime sulphur for fungus control. Suffocates such insects as mites, mealybugs, and scales. Not poisonous to warm-blooded animals. Apply five or six weeks before the buds break open in the spring.

Insecticidal soaps: Control pests such as aphids, mealybugs, mites, spiders, and whitefly. It will not harm beneficial insects and breaks down rapidly.

Nicotine spray: Add five cigarette butts to a litre (quart) of water and let stand overnight. Strain and spray on plants infected with bugs. It's powerful stuff—keep it away from children and pets.

Pyrethrum: A botanical insecticide made from the powdered flowers of a type of chrysanthemum, it is used to kill aphids, whiteflies, leafhoppers, and thrips. Harmful to cold-blooded creatures—avoid using near bodies of water. Insecticidal soap and pyrethrum are a lethal combo for insects.

Rotenone: A botanical insecticide that's used on bush fruits, grapes, vegetables, or flowers. Use as a spray or dust to control such insects as spittle bugs and aphids. Can be toxic to fish, humans, and beneficial insects.

Sticky strips: These yellow strips are coated with a sticky substance that traps insects. The yellow colour attracts such insects as leaf miners and whiteflies.

Tree Tanglefoot: A commercially available sticky paste applied to tree trunks. It acts as a barrier to prevent insects such as ants, caterpillars, and cankerworms from reaching leaves, buds, and fruit.

Ladybug

Praying mantis

Parasitic wasp

Beneficial Creatures

Only a small percentage of the insects in your garden are actually pests; many are beneficial. Get to recognize the beneficial insects I've listed here so you're not killing off the good with the bad. I've also included some hints about how to attract them to your garden. Some beneficial insects are available from specialty suppliers.

Green lacewings: Excellent predators. The larvae control aphids, red spider mites, thrips, and mealybugs.

Ladybugs: Adults are voracious feeders, eating such insects as aphids, mites, scales, mealybugs, leafworms, leafhoppers, and stinkbug eggs.

Parasitic wasps: Trichogramma wasps are small parasitic wasps that attack such insects as the fruitworm, cutworm, tent caterpillar, codling moth, and spruce budworm. They are available commercially as eggs. As adults, they will lay their eggs in the insect and develop in its body, causing its destruction.

Praying mantis: The young eat aphids and leafhoppers; the adults eat such insects as cinch bugs, beetles, crickets, and caterpillars. Can also be purchased.

Don't forget about welcoming birds — great insect eaters — to your garden by providing birdhouses, birdseed, and bowls of water year-round. Other beneficial creatures are snakes and toads. Snakes will be fairly rare in an urban garden, but toads appear as if by magic if you put in a water garden that's at least 1.5 m (5 feet) in diameter.

Identifying and Controlling Insect Pests

Even if some bad guys stake a claim in your flower bed, you might choose to let the insects have a share of your garden as long as they're not too greedy. But every now and then, you may find that you have to resort to warfare. Here's how to recognize some common pests, and a variety of solutions to deal with them as safely as possible.

Aphids: Aphids are very small 0.25 cm ($^1/_{10}$ inch), with soft, pear-shaped bodies that might be green, brown, black, or pink. In the vegetable garden, look for aphids on potatoes, peppers, tomatoes, cabbage, cauliflower, squash, and cucumbers. In the flower bed, you're likely to find these small flies on snowball bush, spirea, nasturtium, roses, and sweet peas — in fact, expect to find them on just about any plant, including houseplants; they are partial to new growth. If you don't actually see the aphids, you can recognize their presence by a sticky "honeydew" on the affected plant. Spray them off the affected area with a strong stream of water from the hose. Before you try one of the repellents that follow, make sure some natural enemy of aphids, such as ladybugs or praying mantis, is not going to solve the problem for you. If the infestation is severe, you'll have to resort to spraying. Use rotenone, insecticidal soap, or pyrethrum directly on the affected area. Control aphids by a concoction of chopped onions and garlic steeped in water for three days. Spray plants with this mixture. Use the yellow sticky cards described earlier. Garlic or mint will repel aphids, so grow them near plants you want to protect. Nasturtiums will attract aphids from other plants. Onions planted near roses will keep aphids away.

Green peach aphid

Larval cabbage-maggot damage

Cabbageworm

Cankerworm

Adult codling moth

Adult cucumber beetle

Cutworm

Flea beetle

Flea-beetle damage

Grasshopper

Leaf-hopper damage

Leaf miner

Black vine weevil: Depending on species, weevils are brown or grey and can be 1.25 cm (½ inch) long. Body is tear shaped and hard shelled; found mainly on West Coast, where it attacks rhododendrons, ivy, and other broad-leaved evergreens. The affected plant will eventually die. Apply insecticidal soap to soil, where the weevil lives.

Cabbage maggot: The maggot is white with no legs, and about 9 mm (³/₈ inch) long. Attacks all members of the cabbage family — broccoli, cabbage, cauliflower, and Brussels sprouts. Control by hand-picking or hose off with water or insecticidal soap. Spread wood ashes around the base of the plant, which is where the fly lays its eggs. Plant mint, rosemary, or sage nearby as a repellent.

Cabbageworm: The green caterpillar bites holes in the leaves of cabbage, cauliflower, broccoli, kale, Brussels sprouts, celery, lettuce, peas, and spinach. Hand-pick and destroy if the infestation is not too large. Otherwise, use insecticidal soap. Use *B.t.* or rotenone every seven days to control the larvae. Plant thyme, dill, or marigolds nearby as repellents.

Cankerworm: These striped brown-and-green worms are about 2.5 cm (1 inch) long, and are visible when they drop from trees by a silky thread. Seen most often on apple trees, but they can also devastate elms, maples, and oaks by eating the leaves.

Cultivate around the trunk throughout the summer to turn up the pupae for the birds to eat. Apply Tanglefoot around the trunk to prevent the female from climbing the tree to lay her eggs. Control with *B.t.* or rotenone.

Codling moth: Grey with brown bandlike markings, about 9 mm (3/8 inch) long, and their larvae attack apples and pears. Look for large holes with reddish brown edges in the skin of the fruit. Use dormant oil and sulphur spray just before the buds open in spring. Or, mix 15 mL (1 tablespoon) each of brewer's yeast and molasses into 250 mL (1 cup) of water. Pour into an old container from yogurt or sour cream, for example, and hang one or two in the tree.

Cucumber beetles: Yellow with black stripes or spots, it goes after not only cucumbers but also squash, pumpkins, melons, and other gourd plants. Chewed leaves are the first sign, leading to an infection of virus and bacterial wilt. Spray or dust with insecticidal soap or rotenone at first sighting. You can also hand-pick insects.

Cutworms: These caterpillars of various colours — grey, brown, black — have plump, hairless bodies, 2.5 cm (1 inch) long. Any flower or vegetable seedling can fall prey to this indiscriminate night feeder, but it's particularly fond of tomatoes, cabbages, and lettuce. Put paper collars — or open-ended tin cans or frozen-juice cans — around the stems of newly planted seedlings. Even a little fence of toothpicks inserted around the stem can foil cutworms. Or circle the plants with ashes or bran. If these suggestions don't work, spray or dust with insecticidal soap. Plant tansy and marigolds as repellents.

Earwigs: This reddish brown insect, about 2.5 cm (1 inch) long, has pincers that protrude from the abdomen. Damage caused by earwigs shows up in holes on leaves. Earwigs like to hide in dark, small places such as hoses, corrugated cardboard, the folds of crumpled newspaper. You can use any of these as traps, collecting them every morning, then shaking the earwigs into soapy water. To be on the safe side, wear gloves while you're doing this, since they can bite. Other methods include putting a small container of beer in the garden as a trap; sprinkling diatomaceous earth in the areas you want to protect; even leaving containers of soapy water around — they'll drown in it.

Flea beetles: Look for small holes made by these tiny black beetles in the plants of the cabbage family, the potato family, radishes, and turnips. If infestation is not too large, hand-pick. Use garlic spray as a repellent or spray with insecticidal soap, pyrethrum, or rotenone.

Gladiolus thrips: The insects are slender and brown-black and the nymphs are yellow-green. They cause silver spotting on gladiolus leaves and flecked and patchy spots on flowers. Spray with insecticidal soap; dust gladiolus corms before storing in fall. (See entry for thrips on page 150.)

Grasshoppers: The presence of these green jumping winged insects is indicated by holes in leaves and petals. They like corn and anything green. Pyrethrum or rotenone will help control them. Repel with nasturtiums and chrysanthemums.

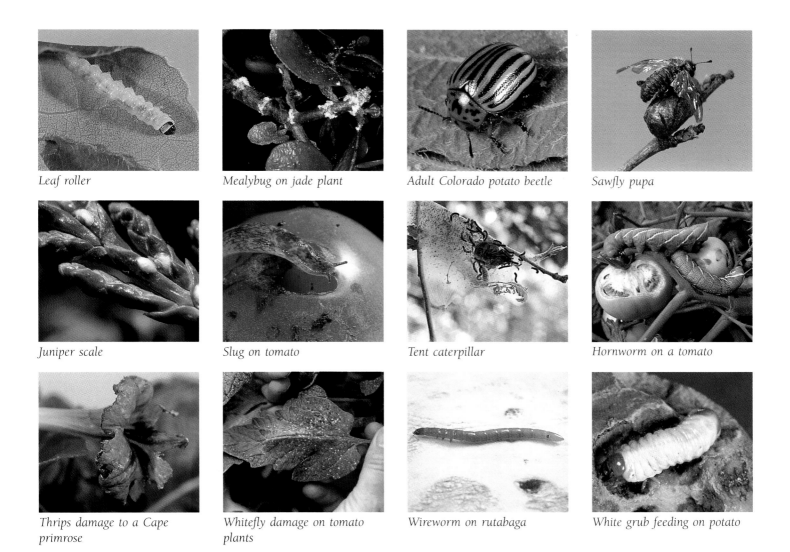

Leaf roller

Mealybug on jade plant

Adult Colorado potato beetle

Sawfly pupa

Juniper scale

Slug on tomato

Tent caterpillar

Hornworm on a tomato

Thrips damage to a Cape primrose

Whitefly damage on tomato plants

Wireworm on rutabaga

White grub feeding on potato

Japanese beetles: The adult beetle is a shiny metallic green with coppery wings, 1.25 cm (½ inch) long; the grub is plump, grey with a dark-brown head, and usually curled up. Beetles attack grape leaves, roses, asparagus, corn, and rhubarb, leaving holes in the foliage. The grubs go after grass roots, causing dead patches on lawns. Control with pyrethrum or rotenone.

Leaf hoppers: These insects are small and green, and usually found on the underside of the leaf; they carry potato viruses. In the vegetable garden, leaf hoppers attack beans, potatoes, and lettuce. In the flower bed, they can be found on many plants, but are especially fond of Virginia creeper, roses, asters, dahlias, and sweet peas. Look for stunted tips and leaves that are curling and turning brown. Spray or dust with insecticidal soap or pyrethrum. Plant nasturtium and marigolds to repel.

Leaf miners: Miners are small maggots or worms, most likely found on birch, elm, lilac, holly, chrysanthemum, columbine, beets, spinach, and chard. They cause dead blotches or create tunnels through leaves. The cure depends on the victim. Columbine: spray with insecticidal soap; birch and elm: spray with insecticidal soap when miners appear, and give birch a second spray in six weeks; lilac: spray when damage first seen; holly: spray late April or early May and three weeks later.

Leaf roller: Colours vary — light to dark green, cream to yellow; caterpillar can grow to almost 5 cm (2 inches); adult moths are no more than 1.25 cm (1/2 inch) long and have brown or grey wings. Gnaws small holes in leaves of fruit trees, chrysanthemums, and other plants. Use rotenone or hand-pick larvae.

Mealybug: Small 6 mm (1/4 inch) insect with flat, oval, greyish white bodies that are covered with a white waxy powder. They are less a garden pest than a houseplant pest. Look for them on leaf axils or on the underside of leaves. Swab the insect with a cotton swab dipped in 50 percent–strength rubbing alcohol.

Mites: Mites are almost invisible — look for fine, silky webbing on foliage. They attack houseplants, roses, azaleas, hibiscus, fuchsia, peaches, strawberries and other fruits, juniper, and spruce, turning the foliage a mottled yellow or grey. Spray with insecticidal soap or wash off with a strong stream of water. Pay special attention to the underside of leaves. Plant garlic near tomatoes as a repellent.

Potato beetles (Colorado beetle): The beetle is striped black and yellow-orange and the larva is orange. They attack potatoes, peppers, eggplants, and tomatoes. Look for holes in leaves. Hand-pick and destroy the bright-orange egg clusters, which you'll find on the underside of leaves, if the infestation is not too large. Otherwise, use insecticidal soap or rotenone, applying the latter every seven days and after rainfalls.

Sawflies: Look for chewed needles and leaves on spruce, balsam, pine, larch, mountain ash, fruit trees, roses, and gooseberries. The damage is done by the yellow-green hairless larvae. Spray with insecticidal soap or rotenone when larvae are visible.

Scale: These scaly insects suck the sap from the plant, causing branches and trunks to dry up. You'll usually see their little rounded bodies firmly attached to the bark of trees or on the underside of leaves of foliage plants; they attack houseplants as well as outdoor plants. Cut out and burn any parts of plants with scale. Use insecticidal soap after eggs have hatched; the dates will vary, depending on the type of scale you're dealing with. Spray trees with a mixture of dormant oil and lime sulphur two or three times before the plant breaks dormancy. Do not spray when plants are in bloom.

Tent caterpillars: Tent caterpillars are hairy and black, with white stripes on their backs; they can take all the leaves off a tree overnight. Their presence is indicated by silky tents in trees. For ornamental plantings, be on the lookout for chewed leaves and flowers as well as the tents. Remove tents by hand at night or cut off the entire branch and dispose of it — but not in the compost. Burning is best if allowed in your area. Spray with insecticidal soap or use rotenone.

Thrips: Thrips are minute insects almost too small to see. If flowers are discoloured or disfigured, shake the plants over a sheet of paper. If thrips have infested them, small dark pellets will drop onto the paper. Thrips suck plant juices, especially in hot, dry weather. Because they like a dry environment, keep plants well misted and watered. In the outdoors, watch especially for their attacks on gladiolus. Indoors, check houseplants. They love flower buds. Spray with Diazinon, pyrethrum, or insecticidal soap. Dust gladiolus corms with sulphur before winter storage.

Potato-beetle damage

Beer for the slugs

Slugs: Holes in leaves in either vegetables or ornamental plants can signal the presence of slugs. Slugs deserve almost a whole chapter to themselves because the methods for dealing with them are numerous! Here are a few that have worked for various gardeners. Wood ashes, talc, lime, diatomaceous earth, or sand sprinkled around plants will help keep them away. Putting out boards near the slugs' favourite plants gives them daytime shelter. Check the boards every day and destroy the slugs. Mulch might be giving slugs a perfect environment. Consider not mulching for a period to see if that discourages them. Hand-pick at night if you have the stomach for it. Slugs are attracted to beer. In the evening, sink a shallow bowl of beer in the garden to the bowl's rim. In the morning you should have dead slugs in the bowl. Keep debris cleared away in the garden; slugs need a cool place to shelter in during the heat of the day.

Tomato hornworms: This large green caterpillar devours tomato leaves. Hand-pick or apply *B.t.*

Whiteflies: You'll know you have whiteflies if a cloud of small white insects flies up from a plant when you shake it. Leaves they've been working on will drop off after becoming discoloured. They're mainly a scourge of houseplants, but they also like tomatoes, fuchsia, chrysanthemums, cucumbers, and hibiscus. Aim the hose at them and wash them off with a strong stream of water. If they persist, spray with insecticidal soap, or use rotenone or pyrethrum once a week for four weeks. You can buy yellow sticky traps to catch whitefies. Plant marigolds as a repellent.

Wireworms: Look for shiny, dark-yellow, wiry worms, but unfortunately the damage is done before you can do anything about them. They attack and destroy underground vegetables, seeds, stems, and roots. Potatoes buried around the garden (mark their location in some way, such as with a stake) will draw the worms and act as traps. Dig the potatoes up every two or three weeks and discard the ones with worms. Replace the discards with new potatoes. Or, use granular Diazinon according to directions.

Some judicious planting can hide a new compost heap.

Time-Saving and Season-Extending Products

June is a satisfying time in the garden. As you savour the fruits of your labour, consider how some nifty products can help you extend the season, reap bigger and better crops, and spend less time on the backbreaking parts of gardening.

Compost Accelerator

An accelerator kick-starts your compost or speeds it up by introducing extra nitrogen, enzymes, and bacteria to the compost. Many commercial accelerators are available; some even promise compost in just fourteen days—a promise to be taken with a grain of salt. However, products such as these are a boon to Canadian gardeners who have to deal with a very short warm season for producing compost. For more information about these accelerators, see my book *The Real Dirt*.

Inoculants

Legumes—plants such as peas and beans—have the ability to take nitrogen from the air, fix it to their roots, and hold it there until it can be used or until it gets ploughed back into the soil. In order for the legumes to extract nitrogen, suitable micro-organisms must be present in the soil. Although these micro-organisms are often present naturally, you can buy an inoculant mix from a seed house or garden centre. Mix the sooty powder with seed before planting so that the coating on each seed is quite thick. Inoculants deteriorate in heat and sun, so it's best to buy a fresh mix each year.

Lawn Dethatchers

I discussed thatch in Chapter 4 and told you about some methods of dealing with it manually. However, you might want to try a commercial liquid dethatcher. It will help the thatch break down, improve the condition of your soil, and let water and nutrients get to the grass's roots.

These dethatchers have only recently been introduced, and have already been proven effective. In my opinion, nothing is easier to use. The products work on the same principle as concentrated compost accelerators by promoting the natural decomposition of the thatch layer that lies below the green portion of grass. They are organic and safe, and they sure beat using a dethatching rake.

Mulching Mowers

You can help your lawn by turning your rotary lawn mower into a mulching machine. Simply buy a special blade that helps throw up and chop into very fine bits the pieces of grass that are cut by the regular blades in your mower. These superfine bits of grass will decompose quickly and add nutrients to the lawn.

Shredders/Chippers

You'll be interested in one of these if you have a lot of brush or thick branches to chip for mulching or putting on the compost. Models of all sizes and capabilities are on the market. Check around before buying one; talk to people who own one. Using them properly can be an acquired knack and you want to be sure you're getting your money's worth out of the purchase. Be sure to invest in safety goggles if you decide to buy a shredder or chipper.

Water Savers

If you do a lot of gardening in containers, water-saving polymer crystals will make your life easier and produce healthier plants. Add the crystals to the soil when you plant. When you water the plants, the crystals absorb the water, releasing it as it's needed. This corrects overwatering and improves soil aeration. You can use the crystals when transplanting seedlings, shrubs, or trees, but not all types can be used for food crops, so check the information on the package carefully before you buy. The crystals of some brands will stay in the soil for three to five years.

Polymer crystals in purchased state (RIGHT OF PHOTO) *and when they've absorbed water* (LEFT OF PHOTO)

The Cold Frame Revisited

By now most of your plants will be out of the cold frame and in their permanent beds until harvesting time. But don't be too quick to think that the frame's use is over until the fall. Adapt the frame as a nursery for young biennials, perennials, plant cuttings from friends' gardens, or hardwood cuttings by replacing the covers with lath, lattice, or shade cloth. Such covers are important to protect plants from the strength of the sun. Let the plants stay in the nursery for the summer before they're planted out in the fall.

In parts of the country with short growing seasons, continue to use the cold frame for starting or growing plants as described earlier. Crops such as lettuce and spinach that bolt in warm weather can be started, hardened off, or even completely raised in cold frames throughout the summer.

Kids' Gardening:
Hummingbird Gardening and Feeding

It's always fun to see birds in your garden — filling up at the feeder, sipping from the birdbath, or scratching around among the plants. But there's nothing to beat seeing a hummingbird darting from flower to flower.

It's possible to attract hummingbirds to your garden without using a special feeder — just let nature do the work! Set off a sunny corner of the garden for your child to grow some plants that hummingbirds like: bee balm, butterfly bush, caragana, cleome, columbine, dahlias, delphiniums, flowering currant, foxglove, gladiolus, honeysuckle, morning glories, nasturtium, petunias, phlox, scarlet runner beans, snapdragons, trumpet vine, zinnias.

These minute birds need a lot of nourishment to keep those tiny wings going, so you might want to provide extra nourishment by putting up a feeder. You can buy hummingbird feeders, of course, but it's more fun to make your own.

Simple Hummingbird Feeder

Make a coil out of wire. It should be large enough to hold a glass or plastic tube, such as a test tube. Insert the tube in the coil, leaving enough space at the bottom for the coil to be placed over a branch or in some other holder. Make a flower shape from some red paper or plastic, and glue it to the top of the tube. Attach the bottom of the coil to a small branch of a shrub. Fill the tube with the hummingbird food (recipe follows) and wait for the hummingbirds to arrive.

Syrup for Hummingbird Feeder: Boil 675 mL (2^1/$_2$ cups) of water in which 175 mL (^{1}/$_2$ cup) of white sugar has been dissolved. Add a few drops of red food colouring if you want. Let the mixture cool before using. Store any unused syrup in the refrigerator. Do not make the mixture any sweeter, because the birds will come to depend on it exclusively. In fact, once the birds know the location of the feeder, you could dilute the mixture with unsweetened water. Like humans, the birds need variety in their diets and if they come to rely on a very sweet syrup, they will suffer from liver damage and possibly a fungus in the mouth.

Change the syrup every week so that it doesn't ferment. While you're replacing the syrup, you should also clean the feeder. Wash it out with water and vinegar, using a scrub brush. If bees or wasps are a problem, coat the feeding hole with a bit of salad oil. Ants can become regular visitors to the feeder, too. Depending on the type of feeder, you can hang it with a thin monofilament fishing line, but I've seen determined ants do a balancing act on this.

It's best to locate the feeder in the shade. Try to keep it away from a window so the bird doesn't crash into it, although if it's near the house, it will be easier to see these entertaining little birds.

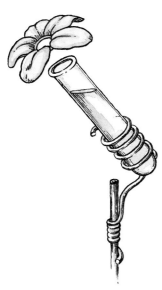

Male calliope hummingbird, which is found in the southwestern part of the country. Ruby-throated hummingbirds are found in the eastern part of Canada in the summer.

June Gardening Checklist

Ornamental Garden

- Feed houseplants and move outdoors to sheltered spot.
- Mow and water lawn regularly.
- Prune evergreens and hedges.
- Take softwood cuttings (see Chapter 9).
- Continue planting bedding plants. Plant out tuberous begonias.
- Mulch beds well to conserve moisture and reduce weeding.
- Plant containers and hanging baskets early in month.
- Stake tall perennials.
- Continue to prune shrubs that have finished blooming.
- Deadhead perennials that have finished blooming. Deadhead annuals to encourage strong bloom.

Fruit and Vegetable Garden

- Treat fruit trees with Tanglefoot to prevent insect pests from climbing trunks. Hang sticky yellow strips to catch apple-maggot flies.
- Prune apples lightly two weeks after blooming. Late in the month hand-thin apples, plums, and peaches.
- Check vegetables for insects and disease.
- Mulch cool-season vegetables to moderate soil temperature.
- Weed asparagus bed when harvesting is complete.
- This month and next, sow fall and winter crops such as rutabaga, Chinese cabbage, collards, endive, and kale. Sow tender vegetables that do not transplant well.
- Plant warm-weather crops to fill the gaps left by harvesting cool-weather crops.
- Transplant eggplant seedlings early in month.

Summer

"**C.** CAN DO BETTER." TYPICAL TEACHER'S COMMENT ON one of my tests in grade school.

I will open this section by making a personal confession: I was an average student from the beginning to the end of my formal years of education. It seems each of my teachers shared the same opinion — that I was an okay student but had the potential to do much better. Every teacher except one. Mrs. Jamieson, grade five. She never scolded me in an effort to drive me harder. Her approach to teaching was to demonstrate, through inspired storytelling, the sheer joy of learning.

Learning became something I did in grade five because Mrs. Jamieson made it so interesting to be a student that you just didn't want to miss the next point.

The summer season in Canadian gardens reminds me of grade five. This is the season during which all your earlier efforts either bloom and bear fruit the way the books describe them, or come up below expectations. This is the season of nurturing earlier investments in sowing, soil preparation, pruning, and pest control.

But more than this, it is the season to experiment with newfound gardening methods (mentioned in this section), and to allow yourself a few failures.

The word *failure* was not in Mrs. Jamieson's vocabulary. And success was not a question of perfect marks or scoring higher on a test than on the previous one. Success was simply expanding your mind by watching, listening, and observing.

I have had summers when my garden didn't deserve better than a C, summers when it rained constantly, and not a single edible tomato was picked. But in following years, I learn to do better, thanks to the many mind-expanding lessons of summer.

Chapter 7

July

Full Flight

The next two months are the most stressful growing months your garden is likely to face. In some parts of the country cool, rainy weather might be causing the blooms of flowers and shrub to turn mushy and unattractive, vegetables and fruit to stop short of ripening, and slugs to have a field day. Other parts of the country may be sweltering from days of unrelieved heat and humidity — good conditions for disease and insects to do their damage. Nevertheless we garden on, undaunted.

The first part of the garden to show the signs of stress in the summer is the lawn.

Summer Care of the Lawn

> **Rule of Thumb**
>
> To tell if your garden needs watering, stick your finger in the soil a few centimetres (a couple of inches) deep. If the soil feels dry, your garden needs watering.

Over the years, I've found that by working hard at my lawn in the spring and fall with fertilizing, aerating, weeding and overseeding, the grass is thick and healthy enough to withstand harsh summer conditions.

If your lawn is looking brown, it's a sign that it's responding to the laws of nature — it's going dormant in a stressful period. One way to keep your grass green during this period is to water infrequently and deeply. A good guide is to water once a week if rainfall has been slight, giving the lawn 2.5 cm (1 inch) at each watering.

If you're going to apply a fertilizer at this time of year, make sure it's low in nitrogen, such as a slow-release 10-6-4. Don't apply it during a drought.

Another way to keep your lawn healthy during the summer is to set the lawn-mower blade high when you cut so that the roots remain shaded.

Watering: If you live in an urban area, all the water that comes out of your hose has gone through a lengthy process of cleansing to make it fit for drinking and other uses around the home. Because of the cost of treating water, it's in the best interests of everyone to use this water sparingly, so let's look at a few watering ideas and systems that will help keep your garden lush and productive while at the same time conserving as much water as possible.

I've already talked about mulching and how it can conserve and retain moisture in the ground. It should be your number-one "watering" technique. But there will be times — for example, when you've just transplanted seedlings — that you will not be able to use mulch or not be able to count on it alone to keep enough moisture in the ground.

*Dappled lawn and healthy
flowers — it's time to enjoy
your hard work!*

First of all, a few notes about watering and some water-saving tips.

❧ Soil with a high humus content will hold more water; clay soils hold three times as much water as sandy soils do.

❧ Not only does clay soil hold more water, it retains water longer than sandy soil.

❧ Soil dries out more quickly on slopes, especially those facing south or west.

❧ Some plants need watering more frequently than others. Know your plants' needs (see the section on vegetables in Chapter 5). Whenever possible, choose varieties that are drought-resistant.

❧ Herbs can withstand very dry conditions. Water only when they begin to droop.

❧ Shallow-rooted crops will need more frequent watering than more deeply rooted crops. Try to plant crops with similar watering needs together. Lettuce, cabbage, and cauliflower are shallow rooted; beans, squash, melons, and peppers have deeper roots.

❧ Raised beds can dry out more quickly than regular beds, usually because they have better drainage. Plants in raised beds are often grown intensively — that is, they are planted more closely together. This has a watering advantage — the closely packed leaves shade the soil — and a watering disadvantage — because there are more plants, they need more water!

❧ For plants such as tomatoes, peppers, and eggplants, make a depression in the soil around each plant. This will act as a small reservoir to catch run-off water.

❧ If plants are drooping in the morning or evening, they need watering. If they droop on a hot afternoon but perk up in the early evening, they're just reacting to the heat.

❧ Climate and weather conditions will affect water needs. Plants and soil dry out quickly in hot, windy weather.

❧ Even though you may be watering less frequently in midsummer, treat seeds and seedlings the same as you would in the spring. If you are sowing second crops, keep the seeds and seedlings well watered. As their leaves develop, gradually cut back on the watering.

❧ Plants that are stressed because of lack of water will produce small, late crops.

❧ Generally, the best time of day to water is the morning, before the sun is at its hottest. The second best time to water is in the early evening.

❧ Water deeply rather than lightly. Deep watering encourages the plants to thrust their roots farther into the soil. The stronger the root system, the greater the plant's access to nutrients and moisture. Plants that are watered shallowly will develop weak roots near the surface of the soil, where they will dry out more quickly.

❧ If you live in an area that suffers from drought, or if you are experiencing a particularly dry summer, save rainwater in a barrel; water at night to lessen evaporation; and, of course, mulch! A friend of mine has come up with an inventive way to recycle water: he has a sump in the basement and has hooked up a flexible pipe in order to direct the pumped water to a particularly dry spot of his garden.

❧ In regions where fall comes early, it's safest to cut back on watering in the late summer so plants can harden off before frost.

Watering Systems

Watering cans: Watering cans are useful for watering specific plants, especially when you're transplanting. You can also more easily avoid watering foliage with a watering can. Choose a can that is rustproof and not too heavy, and has an adequate opening for filling and a good rose. The rose is the part that fits over the spout and does the sprinkling; it should be oval, with many fine perforations to produce a gentle spray, and shouldn't drip.

Hoses, sprinklers, and nozzles: Using a combination of these pieces of equipment is the most common method of watering, but unfortunately it is not the most efficient, even when the system is connected to a timer. It annoys me when people do not set their sprinklers properly and end up watering sidewalks, driveways, and house walls. In times of drought, this is especially wasteful. When you water, you want to get the water into the soil, but with this method, the water falls on the leaves and some evaporates into the air before it reaches the soil. There are a few benefits, though. Because the water falls on the foliage, it cleans it and cools off the plant. This is one type of watering that really should be done in the morning or late afternoon to reduce the amount of water lost to evaporation. Instead of using the sprinkler, you could get a bubbler attachment and move the hose around in the garden after each area has been well soaked. A bubbler disperses the water gently.

Nozzles can produce fine mist to water small plants and gentle sprays to water seed beds. A hard jet of water from the nozzle will knock some insects off plants.

Soaker hoses: One of my gardens is long and narrow, and I find using a soaker hose the most efficient way to water this bed. Some soaker hoses are made of porous materials such as canvas or fibre; some release water through small perforations; other types are made of porous foam or rubber. The water "leaks" gently and evenly out of the hose all along its length so that no water ends up on the foliage of the plant. Soaker hoses can be laid on top of the soil or buried; if buried, freezing should not affect them. Some soaker hoses are so flexible you can weave them among the plants. Install a soaker system early in the season, when it's easier to work around small plants.

Rule of Thumb

Plants that don't like to get their foliage wet are roses, lilacs, zinnias, monarda, phlox, and crops such as melons, zucchini, squash, and pumpkins. They are particularly prone to mildew.

Soaker hose for the impatiens

Giving begonias a gentle spray from a good watering can

Rule of Thumb

It takes at least an hour to soak the plants' root zone in a 3 m by 3 m (10 foot by 10 foot) area using a hand-held hose.

Advantages and disadvantages of various soaker hoses

- Polyester soakers are easy to manoeuvre around plants and release the largest amount of water at one time.
- Some of the rigid vinyl or rubber soakers are hard to lay flat and difficult to bend. A good rubberized vinyl hose won't kink and is much less frustrating to use.
- Polyester, polyethylene, rubber, or vinyl soaker hoses rarely develop leaks at couplings or seams, so they can be left undisturbed for long periods of time.
- Polyethylene and rubber soakers release the smallest amount of water at one time, so they are good for light watering but not for heavy soaking.
- Perforated vinyl soakers are quite durable, but the small holes can become clogged and have to be flushed from time to time. They should also be run at a low pressure in order to prevent erosion.

Drip irrigation: The drip-irrigation system is more expensive to install than the soaker hose but even more efficient. The great benefit is that it gets water directly to the root zone of a specific plant with a minimum of evaporation. The system is usually designed for the individual garden and is made up of a network of small hoses with many small spray heads or dripper heads that are situated near an individual plant. You have great control over the rate at which the water is released and where it will be released. Kits are available so you can install a system yourself, starting small and adding to it over the years. An automatic timer completes the ease of using this system.

Xeriscaping

Xeriscaping is a water-saving method of gardening using drought-resistant plants. The Ontario Ministry of Natural Resources gives the following advice.

- Evaluate your soil. If a handful of soil crumbles when you squeeze it, it will need amendments to help it retain water. Add peat, rock wool, vermiculite, or shredded pine or cedar bark.
- Choose plants that are native to your province and zone, since they are adapted to your conditions and therefore should require less watering.
- Lawns can require heavy watering. Decide if you want to make the size of your lawn smaller by introducing drought-resistant shrubs and ground covers, or select a grass that tolerates dry spells.

Simple Watering Devices

Use these homemade watering systems to deliver water to the root zones of individual plants that require a lot of water. These simple devices also prevent the run-off sometimes caused by surface watering systems.

Earthenware jug:
Bury the container up to its neck next to the plant or plants. Fill with water and cover with plastic or an old saucer to prevent evaporation. Refill when about half empty.

Wine jug:
Choose a jug with a metal screw top. Punch a few holes in the lid, fill the jug with water, and put the lid on. Partially bury the jug, neck down, in the soil next to the plant.

Milk jug:
Make a small slit on one side of the jug near the bottom. Insert some vinyl tubing or wicking material in the hole. Fill the jug with water, then lay the tubing on the soil near the plant, or bury the wick near the root zone.

Cress

SOIL: Cool, rich soil in full sun or partial shade.

SOWING TIME: Ideal for mid- to late-summer planting for fall harvesting.

FERTILIZING NEEDS: Add compost to soil before planting.

WATERING NEEDS: Likes plenty of moisture.

PESTS AND DISEASES: Virtually none.

HARVESTING: Germinates quickly, so you can start harvesting it in about ten days, when shoots are 5 cm (2 inches); or wait until they're 8 to 10 cm (3 to 4 inches) long. It regrows several times; in cool weather, the plant will produce for six to eight weeks.

COMMENTS:

🌱 Sow a crop in the cold frame in the fall for an early spring crop.

Endive, a candidate for the cold frame

Endive and Escarole

SOIL: Cool, moist soil in full sun.

SOWING TIME: Sow outdoors in mid to late summer. In areas with short growing seasons, sow a crop around the end of June for harvesting before heavy fall frosts. Can also be started indoors for transplanting. In a cold frame, they will be edible for most of the winter.

FERTILIZING NEEDS: Fertilize a couple of times during the growing season with fish emulsion.

WATERING NEEDS: Keep soil moist until seeds germinate and until they are a few centimetres (a couple of inches) high.

PESTS AND DISEASES: Virtually none, though in a cold, wet season they may develop rot.

HARVESTING: To extend the season, dig the plants after the first nonkilling frost and plant in tubs of soil in basement or root cellar.

COMMENTS:

🌱 Heat turns both bitter.

🌱 Both are hardy, tolerating light frosts, and will do well in an insulated cold frame.

Kale and Collard Greens

SOIL: Cool soil.

SOWING TIME: Sow kale and collards in ground ten to twelve weeks before the first frost.

FERTILIZING NEEDS: Feed with fish emulsion or other high-nitrogen fertilizer.

WATERING NEEDS: Water well during dry weather.

PESTS AND DISEASES: May be attacked by aphids, cutworms, and leaf miners.

HARVESTING: When they are still young, take the lower leaves of collards and the inner leaves of kale for tender pickings.

COMMENTS:

🌱 A touch of frost sweetens them. Kale can be harvested even when covered with snow. Add a deep mulch when the ground freezes and kale will be ready for harvesting in the early spring.

🌱 Plant in the cold frame about twelve weeks before the first frost for a late-winter harvest.

🌱 Tall varieties are not as hardy as those whose hearts grow closer to the ground.

Kohlrabi

SOIL: Cool, moist, well-drained soil. Does best in soil that is rich in organic matter.

SOWING TIME: Sow in ground ten weeks before first fall frost. Doesn't like to be transplanted.

FERTILIZING NEEDS: Needs good supply of potassium.

WATERING NEEDS: Needs constant, even moisture.

PESTS AND DISEASES: Cabbageworms sometimes attack.

HARVESTING: Harvest when still young; they should be about 6.5 to 8 cm (2½ to 3 inches) in diameter.

COMMENTS:

❧ Can tolerate a few light frosts.

Turnips

SOIL: Cool, moist, well-drained, fertile soil.

SOWING TIME: Sow outdoors in summer eight to ten weeks before first fall frost. Mulch to keep roots cool.

FERTILIZING NEEDS: Likes phosphate; if possible, prepare the turnip bed a season ahead, working in rock phosphate.

WATERING NEEDS: Water deeply in dry weather.

PESTS AND DISEASES: Virtually pest- and disease-free.

HARVESTING/STORAGE: Pick turnips when young for a good flavour.

COMMENTS:

❧ Recommended as a crop for the cold frame.

Decorative Kale: The Hardy Flower That Made Cullen Gardens Famous

My brother Pete has been growing flowering kale and flowering cabbage at our public show garden and miniature village in Whitby, Ontario, for more than ten years. Since he started growing them, the demand for "that beautiful purple cabbage," as people refer to it, has been strong. The great attraction of flowering kale, apart from its fabulous colour, is the fact that it peaks about the second week of December.

It's a showy member of the cabbage family, and although it's edible, it's grown mainly for the rich colours that have attracted so many of our visitors. Its frilly leaves range from creamy white to rosy pink to red. Sow seeds outdoors in the spring in full sun or start indoors four to six weeks before the last frost. You can also buy them as seedlings.

Pruning Fruit Trees and Fruiting Shrubs

When fruit trees and shrubs are young, pruning is carried out to help the plant develop a strong framework of branches. Once the shape has been established and the tree or shrub is vigorous, pruning keeps the interior open and allows moderate growth with good fruit production. Here are some general pruning rules for fruit trees and shrubs, then some advice for specific fruits.

Pruning keeps fruit trees, such as this apple, healthy and productive.

- One general rule seems to be that even experts disagree on the best times to prune! In the following section on individual trees and shrubs, I've tried to give you guidelines and suggestions that represent a variety of opinions.

- Take out branches that are dead, broken, or diseased and those that rub against one another or are in strong competition with one another.

- Remove a whole branch, rather than leaving a stub. An elderly gardener I knew referred to these as coat pegs. He would say you had done a bad pruning job if he could find a peg on which to hang his coat after the branch had been removed.

- Look for branches that droop. They are usually too weak for good fruiting. If these branches are young, shorten them to stimulate growth; if they are old, prune to side branches that are growing in a more horizontal position.

- Don't take more than a third of new growth, whether you're pruning a branch or the whole tree or shrub. If you feel uncertain, restrict yourself to pruning only a quarter of the new growth.

- If a branch has a vertical fork, it's safest to prune out the top part. Leaving the branch unpruned could lead to a complete split when it's loaded with fruit.

- Note where the flower buds form and the age of the wood on which they form. As you prune, keep the flower buds and new shoot growth distributed evenly throughout the tree, making sure that the buds have maximum exposure to the sun. Periodically remove some of the large limbs if it's necessary to get more light into the interior of the tree or shrub.

Apple Trees

- Apple trees bear fruit on wood that is at least two years old.

- The ideally shaped apple tree has a main trunk, with three to five strong, wide-angled branches at about 30 cm (1 foot) intervals up the trunk. A one-year-old tree will have only a main trunk, but pruning it to a height of 60 cm (2 feet) will encourage it to produce several branches in its second summer. For the following two years, prune young trees so that their branches reach upward with tips at least 30 cm (1 foot) apart. Make each pruning cut above a bud.

- Pruning undertaken in the late fall to late winter results in the increase of growth buds, which are small and flat and produce new shoots, rather than the increase of fruiting buds, which are large and round and produce blossoms. Pruning done from midsummer to fall reduces the foliage, encourages fruit buds to form, and restricts growth.

Elderberries

Apricot Trees

- Fruit is set on the spurs formed on second-year growth; these spurs will produce for two to four years.

- If you can grow apricots in your region (you're likely to be in Zone 5 or more), you'll be rewarded with a long-lasting tree that needs little pruning. Just remove dead wood, thin for appearance, and gradually take out the older fruited wood, keeping new growth.

Blackberries

- Blackberries generally bear fruit on one-year-old wood. After the harvest in the fall, remove all the fruiting canes. In the fall, trim remaining branches of the dormant plant to about 1.2 m (4 feet). Remove suckers.

- Removing the flowers in the first season helps establish strong canes and ensure good crops in the future.

Blueberries

- Blueberries generally bear fruit on one-year-old wood.

- Ideally, remove first-year flowers to help plants establish themselves. For the next two years, prune out only dead and damaged branches in the spring. From the fourth year on, take back up to four of the oldest shoots to a new shoot or right down to the soil, again in the spring.

- If you're pruning new growth for shape, do it early in the season so the pruned branches can set buds for next year's fruit.

Cherry Trees

- Sweet cherries bear fruit on wood that is at least two years old. Tart cherries bear fruit on one-year-old wood.

- In the first three years, prune in early spring before growth begins; the aim is to establish the shape of the tree.

- After the first five years, little pruning needs to be done. Just remove dead wood, excess growth, and competing branches in the fall. Be sure that sunlight is getting into the interior of the tree.

Currants

- Currants generally bear fruit on one-year-old wood. Red currants are also borne on wood that is older.

- Currants need pruning every second year. After planting, cut back to 15 cm (6 inches) above ground level, leaving four buds on the shoot. In four years' time, prune again in the autumn, leaving six healthy canes per bush. Every two years thereafter, cut back one-third of the old wood as low as you can.

Elderberries

- In the first year, cut out weak growth and cut back the main shoots to several centimetres (a couple of inches) to a strong outward-facing bud.

- In subsequent years, take out dead wood and overgrown branches. Prune out about a quarter of the old wood, cutting back to the base.

TOP LEFT:
Apple
TOP RIGHT:
Red plum
MIDDLE RIGHT:
White plum
BOTTOM:
Pear

Gooseberries

❧ Fruit is borne on new wood as well as on older wood.

❧ Prune to ground level immediately after planting. Remove first-year blossoms. After the first summer, prune to four or six of the healthiest branches, then cut these back to a bud about 15 cm (6 inches) above the rootstalk. Prune in a similar fashion every year in the fall or late winter, making sure that some healthy older canes are left.

Grapes

❧ Grapes bear fruit on the current season's wood. Prune in the spring or late fall, removing shoots that have borne fruit in the previous year.

❧ Pruning practice depends on the method of growing, the variety planted, and the purpose for which the grapes are grown. If you are growing for fruit production, my book *A Greener Thumb* outlines the two training and pruning systems. If you are growing the vine over an arbour for shade or decorative purposes, prune so that side shoots develop every 38 to 46 cm (15 to 18 inches). In the spring, prune side shoots so that ten or twelve buds are left on each one. That will be sufficient for good growth.

Peach Trees

❧ On a one-year-old tree, cut back the central leader to about 60 cm (2 feet) above the ground in the spring when growth buds have appeared. Make the cut just above a bud. Remove all other side shoots except for the top three or four side shoots or buds. In subsequent years, prune in the late winter, taking out branches that cross, as well as any damaged branches. Remove branches that have stopped producing.

❧ This year's fruit is borne on last year's wood. When pruning, take out old wood — wood that's more than two years old — in favour of new wood.

❧ Thin to allow good penetration of the sun to the interior.

❧ Peach wood is brittle compared with the wood of other fruit trees, and the weight of the fruit can cause damaging stress to the branches, so pruning will lessen fruit production but will help the tree remain healthy longer.

❧ Peach trees need more pruning and have a shorter life than other fruit trees.

Root Pruning

Root pruning is a method of pruning that can invigorate a fruit tree that is producing poorly.

Simply push a sharpened spade into the ground around the drip line of the tree to a depth of about 25 cm (10 inches). Don't wiggle the spade as you do this. The cutting action will prune the roots. Feed with superphosphate in the fall and again in the early spring. A mature tree (over 2.4 m/8 feet) should receive about 1 kg (2 pounds) and a shorter tree 0.5 kg (1 pound).

July Gardening Checklist

Ornamental Garden

🌿 Check mulches on perennials and renew as necessary.

🌿 Apply low-nitrogen fertilizer to lawn.

🌿 Prune deciduous shrubs after flowering.

🌿 Water hanging baskets and containers every day.

🌿 Deadhead annuals, perennials, and roses. Pinch back straggly annuals.

🌿 Lift and divide crowded iris.

🌿 Take semihardwood cuttings for propagating (see Chapter 9).

🌿 Pinch back chrysanthemums and asters again.

🌿 Cut delphiniums to ground after first flowering.

🌿 Plant autumn-flowering bulbs (see Chapter 8).

🌿 Take geranium cuttings.

🌿 Renew mulches as necessary, especially during hot weather. During prolonged wet weather, pull back mulches from plants to discourage mildew and fungus diseases.

Fruit and Vegetable Garden

🌿 In strawberry patch, take out plants that have borne fruit for three years. Remove runners.

🌿 Prune out fruit canes that have been harvested — for example, prune July-bearing raspberries right after their harvest.

🌿 Prune fruit trees and soft fruits.

🌿 Continue to sow such vegetables as lettuce, peas and snow peas, leeks, beans, beets, carrots, radishes, cauliflower, spinach, broccoli, Swiss chard, and turnips. Sow cool-weather greens for fall harvesting. Be prepared to protect some of these cool-weather vegetables from the sun by using screens.

Chapter 8

August

The Filled-in Canvas

For some people, the garden in August can be a disappointment. Suddenly everything seems to have finished flowering and the garden looks a bit bedraggled. Perhaps your plans have not worked out exactly as you had imagined.

Just as winter is a good time to see the bare bones, August shows you the filled-in picture. With those two memories, assess what worked and what didn't. The coming fall is a good time for moving and dividing plants, so begin on next year's garden now. Some of my most creative moments as a landscape designer came during August, when I could look at established gardens and evaluate the whole picture, then steer my clients in the right direction for the following year.

If your concern is the lack of colour at the moment, be assured that it's not necessary for the glory to be over. If you've been deadheading, you should be rewarded with another, though perhaps smaller, burst of blooms just about now. In Chapter 4 I told you about some perennials that provide colour for longer than the usual two or three weeks. In this chapter I'll review some perennials that bloom in August and into the fall, and discuss summer-flowering bulbs. Use this information to start making your plans for next year!

Late-Summer and Fall Perennials

If you want to boost the number of late-summer and fall flowers, plan on giving over no more than a third of the border or bed to them. Keep them balanced with spring and summer flowers for a lush look in three seasons. As with other plantings, spread these throughout your garden in neighbouring drifts for the most attractive impact.

Asters (Aster)

Asters come into their own in the late garden, with flowers from white to pink to purple and even crimson red. You can also choose from a variety of heights — 15 cm (6 inches) to 1.8 m (6 feet). They prefer moist, well-drained soil in full sun and don't like the hot prairie summers particularly; they're susceptible to mildew, especially in dry soil. Divide them every four or five years in the spring. If you pinch the tall varieties when they're about 60 cm (2 feet), they will branch and flower better, but later. To Zone 5.

By August, the butterfly bush
(ABOVE) will have put on
amazing growth; mums usher
in the early-autumn garden.

Baby's Breath (*Gypsophila paniculata*)

Here's a drought-tolerant, hardy member of the garden that flowers from July to September and reaches 90 to 120 cm (3 to 4 feet). Its tiny flowers are white or pink. Once it's been planted, it's difficult to transplant because of its taproot, so be sure of where you want it. It likes sun. To Zone 2.

Black-eyed Susan (*Rudbeckia fulgida*)

This cheerful yellow daisylike flower will bloom for many weeks at the end of the summer and into the fall. It reaches about 75 cm (30 inches) and likes moist, well-drained soil in full sun or light shade. To Zone 4.

Boltonia (*Boltonia*)

An easy-to-grow plant covered with tiny white or pink daisies, boltonia will grow to 1.2 to 1.8 m (4 to 6 feet) and bloom in the late summer and early fall. Because it can be sprawly, plant it at the back of the border where other plants can support it or where stakes won't be so obvious. Give it full sun. To Zone 4.

Chrysanthemum (*Chrysanthemum*)

A traditional sight in many fall gardens, mums are fairly heavy feeders, but as they begin to bloom in the fall, you'll be glad you invested a bit of extra effort in their cultivation. Plant them in full sun in rich, well-drained soil. For more prolific blooms, pinch them when they're about 15 cm (6 inches) and again when the new shoots are 15 cm (6 inches). Depending on the variety, they can be anything from 45 cm (1½ feet) to as much as 1.5 m (5 feet) tall. In Zone 5, give them a mulch to protect them over the winter and divide them in the spring if necessary. To Zone 5.

Goldenrod (*Solidago*)

Contrary to what many believe, goldenrod does not cause hay fever (ragweed does), but its blooming period coincides with all that sneezing and wheezing. It's quite undemanding—it likes sun, but will grow in partial shade, and likes moist soil, but is tolerant of a wide range of soils. Try it near asters for a stunning display of fall colours. Some varieties can be invasive, so look for the ones that grow only 60 cm (2 feet); they won't be as assertive. To Zone 2.

Monkshood (*Aconitum*)

Look for varieties such as *A. carmichaelii* and *A. napellus* if you want fall blossoms. The plant is tall (1.5 to 2.4 m/5 to 8 feet, depending on variety), with blue spires, and likes filtered light, but will grow in full sun if the soil is moist. All parts of the plant are poisonous, but the roots are especially so. To Zone 2.

Sneezeweed (*Helenium*)

Another easy-to-grow late bloomer with daisylike flowers. It blossoms in rich bronzes and reds and clear yellows for four or five weeks. Water it well, plant it in full sun, and it will grow to 1.2 to 1.5 m (4 or 5 feet). To Zone 2.

Goldenrod (ABOVE) *won't make you sneeze — in fact, it's an attractive addition to the back of the border. Every year there seems to be a wider choice of chrysanthemum colours. They make a good replacement for annuals that are showing the effects of a long summer.*

Butterfly bush in bloom

Windflower *(Anemone)*

Look for *A.* x *hybrida* (also known as Japanese anemone) for planting in the autumn garden. Not only are they stunning, if you cut them just as they are beginning to open, they will provide long-lasting cut flowers. Their colours range from white to clear pink to mauve, and are beautifully set off by the silvery green foliage. Grow them in full sun or, preferably, dappled shade; soil should be rich, with lots of humus. Lift in fall when flowering has finished and store over the summer if you're growing them anywhere colder than Zone 6. On the other hand, you can tempt Mother Nature by mulching them heavily to see if they'll overwinter. To Zone 5.

Fall Foliage and Accent Plants

Don't confine yourself to flowering plants for a pleasing fall garden. Consider using plants with colourful and attractive foliage to liven up your border, as well as shrubs and vines for accents.

Artemisias *(Artemisia)*

Artemisias's silvery leaves can help cool down some of the bright autumn yellows and bronzes and link them with the pretty pinks and wines of various fall-flowering plants. It likes full sun, but is otherwise quite undemanding. You can choose from a wide range of heights, depending on the variety — anything from 25 cm (10 inches) to 1.8 m (6 feet). Some varieties are quite vigorous and can take over, but because of their usefulness in the garden at any season, many people forgive them. To Zone 2.

Butterfly Bush *(Buddleia)*

The pale-green foliage of this shrub sets off its purple, rich burgundy, pink, blue, or white trusses to perfection. Add to that the butterflies that flock to the bush in the late summer and you won't find a prettier sight. Cut it back hard in early spring and it will respond with new growth in an amazingly short time. Another, less severe, pruning in midspring will result in larger flowers. Their height varies from 1.2 m (4 feet) to 4.5 m (15 feet). To Zone 5.

Clematis *(Clematis)*

One of the most popular vines has among its many varieties some that bloom in the late summer and early fall. *C. serratifolia, C. tangutica,* and sweet autumn clematis (it's confusingly known by at least three other "official" names — *C. maximowicziana, C. paniculata,* and *C. digitata*) — are three late-flowering varieties to search out. Late-blooming clematis come in a range of colours similar to their earlier relatives — red, pink, purple, and yellow. Plant them in the fall for blooming next fall. A bonus from many clematis are the lovely fuzzy seed heads that remain after flowering. Hardiness depends on by variety; some are hardy to Zone 3.

Summer- and Fall-Flowering Bulbs

As you review your ornamental garden, see if there are spots for some summer-flowering bulbs next year. Plan to plant these bulbs when the ground has warmed up next spring. You'll have to lift the tender bulbs each fall before the soil gets cold, but don't look on this as a chore. The bulbs give you flexibility in your garden design every year, and guarantee spectacular blooms.

For all these bulbs, make sure they have soil with good drainage, water deeply, and use mulch to keep their roots cool and to retain the moisture.

Acidanthera (*Acidanthera*)

This gladioluslike plant gives off an intense spicy fragrance, produces long-lasting, star-shaped flowers in the late summer, and grows to about 90 cm (3 feet). Plant 8 to 10 cm (3 to 4 inches) deep in full sun or filtered shade when the ground is warm. If there's no rain for a week, give it a good watering. Lift in the fall and repot, or store as for gladiolus.

Clematis

Rule of Thumb

To ensure repeat blooming for many years in your gladiolus, don't pick too many leaves when you're cutting the flowers for indoor flower arrangements. Why? Because leaves are the food factory of the bulb.

It seems as if an endless array of begonias is available. They'll do best in a cool, damp spot.

Dahlias thrive in cool summer air and are worth the small effort of lifting them after the first killing frost.

Autumn Crocus *(Colchicum)*

The pink, white, violet, or lilac flowers seem to appear from the bare ground in the fall. In fact, their foliage grows up in the spring and dies down in the summer, so this fall-flowering corm is best planted amid a low ground cover; it will reach 45 to 60 cm (1¹/₂ to 2 feet) in height. Plant 8 to 10 cm (3 to 4 inches) deep in August for late September blossoms and then leave in the ground year-round. It likes full sun and well-drained, fertile soil. A bonus is that squirrels don't like the bulbs. Be aware, however, that the bulbs are poisonous. To Zone 5.

Begonias *(Begonia)*

Tuberous begonias require dedication from the gardener, but they will repay you with fabulous flowers from late June to September when planted in a cool, damp spot. The choice of begonia can be almost overwhelming — single, semidouble, double flowered; forms ranging from camellia, rose, ruffled; in white, yellow, pink, shocking reds and oranges. Heights vary, as well — anything from 20 to 60 cm (8 to 24 inches).

Start indoors in pots in March or April, using moist potting soil and placing the hollow side of the tuber up and the rounded side down. Keep the soil moist, not wet, in a temperature range of 16 to 19°C (61 to 68°F). When tubers sprout in about six weeks, replant in pots three times the diameter of the tuber. When frost is unlikely, put outside in the pots or plant 5 cm (2 inches) deep in a sheltered spot with dappled shade and good air circulation to prevent stem rot. Protect the soft stems from wind damage by staking the taller ones.

In the fall, after the first frost, withhold water for the potted plants and dig the planted ones, letting as much soil as possible adhere to the roots. In about three weeks, take off the wilted foliage from the potted tubers and just leave the tubers in the pot; put the dug tubers in a container of dry vermiculite or peat moss and store in a room with a temperature between 5 and 10°C (40 and 50°F).

Caladium *(Caladium)*

It's nice to know that there's one plant that likes hot, humid summers. You can brighten a shady corner with the colourful, heart-shaped foliage caladiums produce or grow these tolerant plants in a sunny spot; they are about 30 to 45 cm (1 to 1¹/₂ feet) high. You can plant them directly in the ground (to a depth of 5 cm/2 inches), but they lend themselves to container growing in a mix of equal parts good garden soil and peat moss. If grown in containers, just bring indoors for the winter at the end of the season. If planted in the ground, dig them before the first frost, removing most of the clinging soil. Dry them for a week or so in a warm, dry place before storing at 16 to 21°C (65 to 70°F) in a box or paper bag with dry vermiculite, peat moss, or sawdust.

Cannas *(Canna)*

These tender rhizomes are most frequently seen in public plantings, but miniature varieties can easily be incorporated in the home garden. Their flowers, similar to lilies, come in soft yellows, apricots, pinks, and reds, and grow to 60 cm (2 feet). They'll start blooming in midsummer and continue to the fall. Pot up rhizomes indoors in

March or April and move to a sunny, well-drained spot after the last frost, adding a 5-10-5 fertilizer. Continue fertilizing every couple of weeks and keep watered in dry weather. After the first frost, cut down stalks, lift the rhizomes, and dry for a few days. Sprinkle with sulphur, pack stem side down in dry peat moss or vermiculite, and store in a cool (7 to 10°C/45 to 50°F) dry place.

No garden should be without day lilies. Individual blooms last only a day but there are always more to open.

Dahlias *(Dahlia)*

This is an easy tuber to grow in the northern parts of the country because dahlias like the cool summer air. They come in a wide variety of sizes and colours. In May or June, plant the tubers outdoors, about 5 cm (2 inches) deep, in well-drained, rich soil that gets full or partial sun. The tubers are planted horizontally with the sprout pointing up. If you've got tall varieties, spring is the time to insert a stake so that you don't damage the tubers at a later stage. At planting time, feed with 6-12-12 and bone meal. They're heavy feeders, so give them another light fertilizing a few weeks later. Keep them well watered when they start blooming in late summer and deadhead frequently.

Store cleaned dahlia tubers in a dry medium.

Dig them up after a killing frost, knock off soil, and let dry in the sun for a few hours. Dust with sulphur and store in a dry, cool place in a box or plastic bag of vermiculite, peat moss, sawdust, or sand; temperature in the room should range between 2 and 10°C (35 to 50°F). Check them now and again, and if they have started to shrivel, add a little water; if they have some growth, open the container to let some of the moisture evaporate. Divide them in the spring when bud growth starts.

Rule of Thumb

In the fall, lift cormlets
(also called cormels)
and clean them — dust
with garden sulphur
and surround them with
vermiculite in a porous
container. Store in a cool,
dark place.

Gladiolus (*Gladiolus*)

This corm likes rich, well-drained soil in the full sun. Plant in May about two weeks
before the last frost, 10 to 15 cm (4 to 6 inches) deep, fertilize with 6-12-12 and
keep well watered — the water should be applied to the roots, not via a sprinkler.
Prairie gardeners would be well advised to grow early to midsummer glads because
of the short growing season.

The ruffled blooms, which come in a wide range of colours, appear in late July
and continue for about two weeks, but if you practise succession planting, you should
get blooms until the fall. Gladiolus benefits from staking.

When the leaves turn brown, dig up the corms and remove the foliage. Harvest
the new corms and discard the old ones. Let the new corms dry in a shady spot until
the soil flakes off, then treat with a fungicidal bulb dust before storing them in mesh
bags in a cool — 2 to 7°C (35 to 45°F) — dry, dark place. Don't plant glads in the
same place more often than once every four years.

Lilies (*Lilium*)

By choosing your varieties carefully, you can have a lily in bloom from June right
through the summer. Some of them grow fabulously tall, so you're best to put them
at the back of the border. Plant the bulbs 5 to 15 cm (2 to 6 inches) deep in well-
drained soil as soon as the soil can be worked. They can stay in the ground over
winter, but to be safe, mulch the bulbs for the first few years. Generally, they like full
sun, but will tolerate some shade.

If you don't have a good showing from your lilies the first season, don't despair.
It takes them a season to build up their roots. However, once they've settled in, they'll
last for years. Divide them every few years if they seem less productive.

*A few lilies will provide a
heavenly scent on the summer
air.*

Bulb Terminology

The term *bulb* is used to describe not only true bulbs but also corms, tubers, tuber-corms, and rhizomes. Their common element is that they all store their food underground in a swollen structure (the bulb, tuber, or rhizome). Their differences are more obvious and are described in the sections that follow.

Bulbs

At the bottom of the bulb is a base plate — the underground stem — from which the roots issue. Once a bulb has finished blooming, it starts to store nutrients for next year. The leaves provide the food that nourishes the bulb while this process goes on, so it's important to leave the bulb's foliage on the plant, even though the blooms have faded.

Bulbs include alliums, fritillarias, muscari, tulips, daffodils, scilla, snowdrops, chionadoxa, hyacinth, and lilies.

Tubers

The tuber — storage tissue that grows close to the surface of the soil — produces roots and stems from growing points rather than from a base plate. Buds and new tubers grow near the base of the stem and fibrous feeder roots take in the nutrients to feed the plant.

Unlike bulbs, tubers are not hardy, so they have to be lifted in the fall. When lifting tubers for winter storage, make sure a small section of the stem is still attached. Store in a dry, cool place.

Tubers include the Peruvian lily, ranunculus, and dahlia.

Corms

Most corms, unlike bulbs or tubers, die after blooming, but new corms grow from the lateral bud or buds they produce. The bud has a root that issues from the base plate and growing points from which leaves and flowers issue. The corm itself — the part that is underground — contains the food that produces a new flower and that will nourish the new corm.

Tender corms need to be lifted each fall. Break off the new cormlets and discard the spent mature corm.

Corms include crocuses, dogtooth violet, acidanthera, freesia, and gladiolus.

Tuber-corms

Tuber-corms are disc shaped, with buds on top and roots on the bottom. They grow larger as they age, but do not produce offspring.

Tuber-corms include anemones, begonias, cyclamens, and gloxinias.

Rhizomes

Like a corm, a rhizome is actually an underground stem of storage tissue, which grows just under the surface of the soil. The roots grow down from the bottom of the rhizome and stalks and leaves grow from eyes or buds on the upper part.

Rhizomes include day lilies, bearded irises, lily of the valley, cannas, and agapanthus.

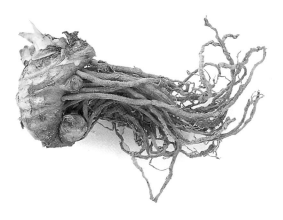

Lily of the Nile (*Agapanthus*)

The showy starlike flowers of this fragrant rhizome come in blue, violet, or white in the late summer and are borne on strong stems. Rhizomes are potted up indoors in the spring. After the last frost, move outdoors to a warm sunny position, where the plant will grow to 1 m (3 feet). In the fall, bring them in for overwintering in pots, watering them occasionally; or store in the same fashion as dahlias.

Ranunculus (*Ranunculus*)

This tuber produces flowers with tightly packed petals the texture of tissue paper. Their full, round heads blossom in white, yellow, orange, pink, or red. Plant tubers 5 cm (2 inches) deep with their "claws" facing down. You'll get five or six weeks' worth of bloom in early summer. It likes cool weather and a sunny spot in the garden. Lift in the fall and store in peat or perlite over the winter at 10 to 13°C (50 to 55°F).

Summer Hyacinth (*Galtonia*)

A beautiful addition to the back of a sunny border (it grows to 1.2 or 1.5 m/4 to 5 feet), summer hyacinth produces white, bell-shaped blossoms that are fragrant and long-lasting. It likes rich, well-drained soil. Plant the bulbs 15 to 20 cm (6 to 8 inches) deep. In the mildest regions of the country, plant in the fall; in all other regions, plant out in the late spring. In the fall, lift the bulb before frost hits, dry and clean it, and store it for the winter at a temperature of about 15°C (60°F).

Grass

As you contemplate your garden at this time of year and make notes of bare spots in the late-summer border, don't overlook grasses in your design plans. By planting even one type of grass, you can add colour, movement, and life to a garden. Some grasses will keep on giving right through the winter. Eulalie grass (*Miscanthus*) is a tall graceful plant that over the fall and winter becomes a rusty orange, burgundy, or silvery beige, depending on the variety. Its strong stems stand up to wind and wet snow. Plume grass (*Erianthus ravennae*) carries silver-white flowers in late September, turning brown over the winter. Silver spike grass (*Spodiopogon sibiricus*) has leaves similar to reeds (which might explain why it likes moist or even wet soil). It turns from green to red to gold by the fall and stays attractive well into the winter.

Revisiting the Cold Frame

August is a good time to renew the soil in your cold frame. This should be done every two or three years for permanent cold frames. If you've grown mainly crops of the cabbage family in the cold frame, the soil should be changed every year.

Dig out the top 10 to 15 cm (4 to 6 inches) of soil and mix it with compost and composted manure. Put this back into the frame, adding any leftover soil to the compost pile. Rake the surface smooth and it will be ready for new plantings.

At this time of year, you may want to set a portable cold frame over slow-to-ripen, heat-loving crops, such as melons, to encourage them to mature and ripen.

Some grasses for late summer interest: silver spike grass (TOP LEFT); *Hokonechla macra* (TOP RIGHT); *fescue* (MIDDLE RIGHT); *eulalie grasses* (BOTTOM RIGHT AND LEFT).

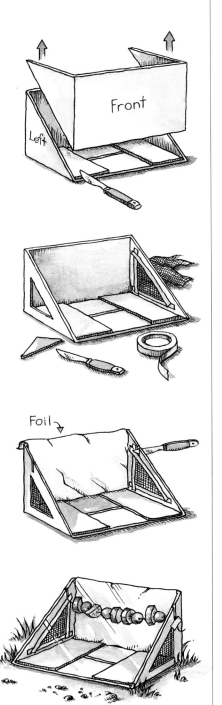

Kids' Gardening:
Making a Solar Dryer*

Whether you use produce from your child's garden, your garden, or the local supermarket, building this solar dryer and then drying food for snacks or cereal or ice-cream toppings is great fun.

Cut the top flaps off a rectangular cardboard box. A box about 25 by 40 cm (10 by 15 inches) and 20 cm (8 inches) deep is a good size. Label all the sides: back, front, left side, right side, and bottom.

Using a ruler and pencil, draw a line from the back top corner to the lower front corner on both sides. Cut along the lines and across the bottom front. You don't need this front section, so set it aside.

In the left and right sides, cut a triangular window, and on the inside of the box, cover the window with a layer of cheesecloth, gauze, or similar light fabric. Seal the edges of the fabric to the cardboard to prevent any small flies from entering.

In the top left side, make a vertical slit about 4 cm (1½ inches) deep and about the same amount from the back. Do the same for the right side.

Cover the inside back with a piece of aluminum foil, using tape, if necessary, to hold it in place.

Gather the fruit you want to dry—apples and grapes are good for the first attempt at drying. Slice them thinly and thread them on a piece of string, using a darning needle. Stretch the string between the left and right sides, sliding it into the vertical cuts and taping or knotting the ends on the outside.

Cover the dryer with plastic wrap, sealing it along all edges. Use tape if necessary.

Put the dryer in a sunny window or outside in a sunny, protected spot. Bring it indoors at night. In two or three days, the fruit will be dry.

Experiment with other kinds of fruit, such as bananas.

* Adapted from *The Kids Cottage Book* by Jane Drake and Ann Love (Toronto: Kids Can Press, 1993).

August Gardening Checklist

Ornamental Garden

- Make note of spaces in garden that need filling; compile list of plants to add to provide continual blooming or foliage interest.
- Continue with deadheading of annuals, perennials, and roses.
- Fertilize plants in containers and hanging baskets.
- Take cuttings of geraniums and alpines, such as dianthus (see Chapter 9).
- Take root cuttings of perennials for propagating (see Chapter 9).
- Take cuttings of shrubs such as camellia, weigela, and butterfly bush (see Chapter 9).
- Collect seeds of plants you want to propagate.
- Prune climbing roses.
- Prune vines to control growth.
- Plant or divide irises if not already done.
- Plant more fall-flowering bulbs.
- Clip lavender as flowering finishes.
- Stop watering roses to slow growth in preparation for winter.
- Give annuals such as petunias and lobelia a hard pruning to revive them.

Fruit and Vegetable Garden

- Cut out old raspberry canes if not done in July.
- Clean out the cold cellar, putting old vegetables on the compost pile. Wash with household bleach and water, scrubbing with a brush to remove any mould. Whitewash interior walls if you desire.
- Renew soil in cold frame.
- Continue to sow late-season crops such as lettuce, carrots, Swiss chard, kale, beets, mustard greens, spinach, corn salad, turnips, and Oriental greens.
- Divide established clumps of chives and shallots.
- Start seeds of herbs for indoor growing—basil, dill, parsley.

Zones 7 to 9

- Sow broad beans for late-fall harvesting.

Chapter 9

September

Extend the Season

The kids are back at school, the days are getting shorter, the evenings are turning nippy. Change is in the fresh autumn air and it's time to start thinking about when that first frost is going to hit the garden and how to prepare for it. Often after the first frost there are many sunny, warm, productive days, so it's worth a bit of effort to protect plants. It's also time to bring in some of that harvest, so I'll give you some hints about keeping produce as fresh as possible for as long as possible. As well, I'll talk about propagating, a fun aspect of gardening that can make you feel like a real professional. And it's not too early to be thinking ahead to next spring—and that means bulbs!

Extending the Fall Season

Don't let the first frost signal the end of your garden, especially if the cold snap comes unusually early for your area. The weather is bound to improve, and you can have many days, if not weeks, of additional bloom from flowers and crops in the vegetable garden.

At the first hint of frost, pick all the ripe crops and store them in a basement or garage. Crops that aren't ripe yet should be covered with sheets, blankets, rugs, or comforters. Do this in the late afternoon, when the soil is at its warmest, and take off the covers the next morning.

Ripening Late Produce

There probably isn't a gardener in Canada who hasn't had his or her heart broken by seeing unripened tomatoes go to waste at the end of the season. Here are some ideas for ripening a variety of crops that won't make it without some help. Note that they will not increase in size, and if they are not sufficiently mature, they will rot.

- Pull out tomato vines and hang in a shed.
- Pick off the larger tomatoes and spread them on a sunny windowsill.
- Put unripened tomatoes in a warm, dark place to ripen (I know this seems to contradict the previous suggestion, but each method has its adherents!).
- Apples, pears, plums, and elderberries will keep ripening after being picked.
- Pumpkins will sometimes ripen—or at least turn yellow—on a sunny windowsill.
- When snow starts to fall, pull up the stalks of Brussels sprouts and bury their roots in a box in the cold cellar or basement for continued harvesting.

Time to lift the gladiolus in preparation for winter storage (ABOVE). *I could have left these a little longer to continue enjoying their colour, but many annuals are still blooming* (BELOW). *The perennial sedum 'Autumn Joy'* (FAR LEFT) *is just beginning to come into its own.*

Transplant peppers to continue growing indoors.

🌱 Peppers and eggplants will not continue to ripen once picked. However, you can dig up your pepper plant and bring it indoors. It can keep producing fruit until late in the year if it's in a sunny spot. Treat it as a potted plant and put out again late the next spring.

Making the Most of Your Crop

No matter how careful you are in planning succession plantings, choosing varieties that mature at different times, and controlling the amount you grow, somehow there comes that week or so when everything is ripening at once. What are you going to do with it all? If you've got more than you're likely to eat even if the entire harvest is preserved, invite friends and neighbours to help themselves — make it a party! A seniors' housing complex that I've given some gardening advice to has plots for vegetable growing. One person grows a bumper crop of cabbage and shares the whole crop with others. Someone else grows lots of tomatoes, and shares accordingly. It's a great system!

Although most food banks don't take fresh produce, you might be able to find a local charitable organization that can use your bumper crops. But before you do that, of course, you will want to preserve as much as you can in a fresh state.

The Cold Cellar

In this age of highly insulated houses, not many of us have cold cellars in our basements. But as interest in growing our own vegetables and preserving them increases, so, too, are we seeing the return of the cold cellar — in our grandparents' time it was called a root cellar. Today people have to have a cold room built, since most basements are probably too warm, but you can use cold places throughout the house as storage spots. You might have an uninsulated pantry, front or back vestibule, closet, or area under some stairs that could make do as a cold cellar.

If you use your basement for produce storage, too much humidity may be a problem, rather than too little, but if it is dry, keep pans of water or wet sand in the room to prevent the produce from becoming dehydrated. Air circulation is important to prevent mildew, particularly in the summer. Wash off any mildew on walls with a stiff-bristled brush and a solution of household bleach and water. Ideally, the basement will have a window that can be opened during the spring, summer, and fall. If there isn't a window, install a vent that you can control to allow warm air to leave and cool air to enter.

Different crops have different storage needs, but since you will probably have only one room available to store all your produce, you will have to accommodate a variety of these needs. Don't despair — it's not that hard. Most produce has to be stored in cool, moist or cold, moist conditions — just above freezing is best. Shelves built at different levels will provide a range of temperatures. Keep a humidity gauge and a thermometer in the cold cellar; two thermometers would be perfect, one at the top level of storage and the other at the lowest level of storage.

🌱 Store root vegetables in boxes or bags if you have a good level of humidity — in the range of 90 to 95 percent. Install a meter to measure humidity if you're unsure about the level.

🌱 Other containers for storage are plastic boxes, woven plastic bags, plastic pails.

🌱 Ideally, the cold cellar should be dark. If you have a window, cover it over.

🌱 Apples, beets, and kohlrabi do well on a low level, where the temperature is coolest — about 0°C (32°F) is perfect.

🌱 Potatoes, carrots, radishes, and beets like a warmer temperature — from 2 to 4°C (35 to 40°F) — and should be stored on higher shelves.

🌱 Fruits and vegetables with a high water content, such as tomatoes, peppers, and squash, should be kept at the top level in the cold cellar, at a temperature of more than 4°C (40°F).

🌱 Beets, carrots, potatoes, and turnips can be packed in sand, sawdust, or peat. It's important to keep potatoes well covered so they don't turn green. Dampen the medium slightly if your cellar is dry.

🌱 Prevent any bruised produce from touching unblemished produce.

🌱 Remember — don't be in too much of a hurry to harvest completely some of the crops that like a cold snap: Brussels sprouts, and parsnips, for example. They'll withstand cold temperatures, which can actually improve their flavour.

🌱 Garlic, pumpkins, onions, and dried beans prefer low humidity and should be kept in a separate dry location. Store onions in mesh bags.

Storing produce from your garden doesn't need to take up a lot of space. Some of the vegetables above — the tomatoes and peppers, for example — will be used more quickly than others — such as the squash, beets, and carrots.

Other Methods of Preserving the Harvest

Drying: An easy way to preserve some of your harvest is by drying. You can purchase an electric dryer that has an automatic temperature control or buy or construct a solar dryer yourself.

Herbs can easily be dried by hanging bunches in a dry place out of direct sunlight. Good air circulation is important. When they're dry, strip the leaves from the stems and store the leaves in opaque containers.

Some fruits and vegetables dry more satisfactorily than others. Tomatoes are one such crop. Cut small tomatoes into halves and larger ones into thick slices. If you use an electric dryer, they should be ready for storing in glass jars in about twelve hours.

Natural deep freeze: You know by now that snow is a great insulator, but it can be used as a deep freeze, too. I've heard of one gardener who leaves her Brussels sprouts in the ground all winter. She lives in an area that can count on good snow cover every year, so after a few hard frosts, she dismantles the stakes she's used to keep her sprout plants upright and lets them topple over, leaving the sprouts on the stalks. The sprouts freeze and the snow blanket protects them from thawing on sunny days. When she wants sprouts, she just goes out, uncovers the plant, picks the sprouts, and covers the remaining ones with snow again. When the snow cover is less than 15 cm (6 inches), she shovels more snow on to keep the sprouts frozen. Only when the snow cover becomes patchy does she finally pick the sprouts and freeze them the conventional way — sometimes in early March!

Moving Indoors

I find that one of the easiest ways to bring my summer colour indoors is to grow my favourite annuals, like impatiens and petunias, in terra cotta pots on my patio. At the end of the season, I prune them back, treat them with insecticidal soap solution and bring the potted plants into our sunroom. Within a few weeks, we have masses of bloom.

Bedding plants such as marigolds, impatiens, and ageratums are good candidates for this treatment, as are herbs and late-flowering plants. Not only will you have more houseplants, but you will be able to take cuttings in the late winter for next year's garden. And you'll be keeping your thumb green over the winter.

Use a good professional potting soil for best results or mix up your own (see page 199). Most of the plants will like cool temperatures, between 10 and 18°C (50 and 65°F) and bright light from a south-facing window or fluorescent lights.

The pots you use should be slightly larger than the root ball of the plant you're transplanting and should have drainage holes.

Here are some tips about particular plants that can be brought indoors, and their needs. Don't forget to check them all for insects and, if possible, quarantine them for a few weeks in a separate room before exposing them to your other indoor plants. It's not a bad idea to transplant them several weeks before you plan to bring them inside to give them a chance to get used to the new pot. This will also allow you to watch them for any pest or disease problems.

Don't consign annuals to the compost pile yet! Transplanting these lobelia and bringing them indoors will keep them blooming for weeks longer.

Hardwood cuttings: In the early fall or winter, choose stems from that year's growth of plants such as forsythia, mock orange, hydrangea, rose, or lilac. Each stem should be cut into lengths of 23 to 30 cm (9 to 12 inches), making the cuts just above a bud at the top and just below a bud at the bottom. These buds are where the future roots and leaves will form. It's best not to use the tip as a cutting because it will produce weak growth. To stimulate root growth, use a rooting hormone. Plant the cuttings in a pot indoors, using a moist soil mix and making sure that one or two buds are covered, or plant directly in the soil if it's not frozen. Outdoors, the cuttings should be inserted into the soil so that at least half, ideally two-thirds, of their length is underground. In very cold regions, gather the cuttings into bunches and bury them horizontally under 15 to 20 cm (6 to 8 inches) of sandy soil. In the spring, dig them up and, after separating them, plant them, following the instructions given previously. Don't despair if the cuttings have not put on root growth over the winter. Some species will root quickly; others will wait until spring.

Make stem cuttings just above and below a bud.

Use some rooting hormone, then push the cutting into the soil so that two-thirds of the cutting is covered.

Leaf Cuttings: This method of propagation is frequently used with tropical plants and other houseplants. Simply take a mature healthy leaf and on its underside make small cuts where the main veins meet, cutting through the veins. Peg the leaf onto the surface of a pot of sandy compost, cut side down. Weight the leaf with small pebbles, if necessary, and cover the pot with a plastic bag. A new plant will root at each cut in about four weeks. Remove the plastic and leave the pot in a warm, shaded spot for a few more weeks, after which you can pot up the individual plants, carefully separating them from the mother leaf.

African violets will root simply by inserting the stem and leaf in the growing medium, ensuring that the leaf does not touch the growing medium. Water well, put the pot into a plastic bag, and seal the bag with an elastic band. If water condenses on the inside of the bag, remove the bag and put a new one on, or turn the original one inside it and reuse it. Although you want the soil to remain moist, too much moisture will lead to rot.

Another type of propagating by leaf cutting is called leaf-bud propagation. Do it in the late summer or early fall. It can be done for many different plants, especially shrubs. Cut a shoot that began growing the previous spring and that has several leaves. Make the cut about 18 mm (3/4 inch) below the lowest leaf. At the place where each leaf joins the stem — the axil — you should see a growth bud. Make a

Make small cuts on the main veins on the underside of a leaf to propagate many houseplants.

Put the leaf on sandy compost, pegging it so that the cuts on the underside are in contact with the soil.

Small pebbles can be used in addition to the pegs to be sure the leaf is touching the soil.

straight cut just above the bud in each leaf axil. Scrape some bark off the bottom part of the cutting and dip it into some rooting compound. Plant the cuttings in a pot with a mixture of fifty-fifty peat moss and perlite. Each bud should be firmly planted 6 mm (¹/₄ inch) below the surface. Water lightly and cover with a plastic bag as described for softwood cuttings. Put in a cold frame or an unheated room out of the direct rays of the sun for about six months. Repot in individual containers, watering well. These pots then go back to the cold frame or unheated room. Be sure they don't dry out. Shrubs should be ready for planting out in another three to six weeks. Tender plants should be potted up again and put in the cold frame for as long as a year before being planted outdoors.

Propagation by Offsets and Runners

Many houseplants produce offsets—a new rooted shoot sent up by the parent plant—or runners—small rootless plants produced at the end of a long thin stem from the parent plant. Spider plants, ferns, and fibrous-rooted begonia are examples of plants that reproduce in this way. In the spring or fall, remove offsets when they're about half the height of the parent plant and pot them up separately. For runners, detach them from the parent, cut off the long stem, and pot up the new small plant. Since these small plants don't have roots to act as anchors, set the plantlet in a small depression in the pot and firm the soil around the base. Put a plastic bag over the pot as described earlier. Keep the new plants out of direct sunlight. Roots should form in about ten days.

Spider plants produce runners, which can be snipped off.

Set the runner in potting soil and firm the soil around it.

Propagating by Layering

Soil layering: Propagate shrubs by soil layering in autumn or winter. Choose a flexible branch that has grown this year, but has not flowered. Make a small upward cut in the branch at the point that will be rooted; you can also just twist the branch to break the tissue on the surface. Take off the leaves from that section of the branch that will be buried. Bend the branch down to the ground and bury the cut point in a 7 to 10 cm (3- to 4-inch) hole, adding equal parts of peat moss and coarse sand to the hole. It is advisable to stake the branch and pin it securely so that winds or other movement won't dislodge it. Water thoroughly and keep well watered. It may take a year for the roots to develop sufficiently that the young shrub can be separated from the main plant and transplanted to its final planting spot.

I find that gardening is full of pleasant surprises — sometimes propagation by layering happens by accident. One year I inadvertently covered part of a low-lying branch from a dogwood shrub with soil while I was planting some periwinkle. About six months later, pulling up weeds, I discovered that the branch had taken root and I had a new dogwood.

A variation of soil layering is serpentine layering, which is a method of propagating vines to give several new plants. In the late spring or early summer, choose a pliable young stem and make nicks on the underside by each leaf node. Lay the stem on the ground and bury the nodes, leaving the rest of the stem above

Rule of Thumb

Rooting compounds generally stimulate the formation of roots for most plants. English ivy is an exception. Rooting compounds can actually prevent it from rooting.

To propagate by layering, choose a branch that has not yet flowered.

At the point that will root, make a small upward cut; do not cut through the branch.

Bury the nicked section with peat moss and coarse sand in a 50:50 mix.

To protect the branch at it roots, stake it so it won't be dislodged.

ground—it will look like a row of hoops—and two pairs of leaves between each node planting. Add the peat moss–coarse sand mixture to the hole. Keep well watered. By the fall, you should have a new plant rooted at each node. Dig them up, separate them, and replant in a new location.

Air layering: Plants that have woody stems, whether houseplants such as the rubber plant and ficus or outdoor plants such as magnolia and viburnum, are propagated by air layering, either in the spring on mature wood or in the late summer on hardened shoots of the current year's growth. Choose the top of a branch or the tip of the plant. In the first 25 to 40 cm (10 to 15 inches), select a spot just below a leaf node. Take a rather deep slice of wood about 2.5 cm (1 inch) long. Apply rooting hormone to the wound. Wrap and tie a small sheet of plastic just below the wound, making it into a cup shape. Spread several handfuls of moist sphagnum moss around the cut, packing it into the plastic cup and squeezing it fairly tightly around the stem 5 cm (2 inches) above and below the cut. Tie the bag at the top. Check it every week to ensure that the moss is still moist. At any sign of drying, remove the plastic, mist the moss, and replace the plastic. Roots are unlikely to form before ten weeks. When the roots have formed, take off the plastic and cut off the new plant, keeping the peat moss attached to the roots. Plant in a pot and keep in a cold frame for a couple of weeks before starting to harden it off by opening the frame more every day. The new plant can then be planted outdoors.

Make a slanting slice in a branch or stem.

Apply some rooting hormone to the open tissue.

Pack moist sphagnum moss into a small plastic "cup."

Tie the "cup" at the top to keep the moss moist.

In September, spring seems far away. But by planting bulbs now, you'll reap dividends in the spring. If you plan your tulip planting carefully, you can get a succession of blooms over many weeks. Primroses are another spring favourite, though they're not bulbs. If you find some primrose plants on sale late in the season, pop them into a shady, moist spot.

Dreaming of Spring

One of the joys of gardening is looking ahead to the next seasons. This is one of the best times of year for that looking ahead — planting bulbs in the fall for spring enjoyment. Put in some of the old favourites, but try a few of the less well known bulbs, too.

Plant spring-flowering bulbs in the fall to allow them to develop a good root system before the winter freeze-up. Choose bulbs that are firm, have no soft spots, sprouts, mould, and don't give off a bad odour. Good bulbs feel heavy for their size. Plant them in a sunny, well-drained bed and fertilize lightly with special bulb fertilizer at the time of planting and in the spring. Keep the bed well watered.

On the prairies, where spring is often a short season, gardeners should plant bulbs in a site that gets spring sunshine, but is protected from the heat of early summer — the east or west side of a building would be a good choice, so that they are shaded for part of the day. Unfortunately, attempting to grow bulbs in the northern regions of Canada can be a frustrating experience.

Fall-Planted Bulbs for Spring Flowering

Anemone

Rule of Thumb

For the best effect, plant bulbs in groups, or drifts, rather than as individual specimens. I achieve a natural look in my garden by mixing crocus, scilla and dwarf narcissus bulbs in a box, then walking slowly under some trees and throwing the bulb mixture over my shoulder. Wherever they land, I plant. The result — a charming hodge-podge.

Alliums *(Allium)*

This relative of the onion blooms in late spring or early summer in colours of rose, purple, or white, and comes in sizes that range from several centimetres (a few inches) to 2 m (6½ feet). Its flowers and its seed heads are both attractive additions to flower arrangements. It is reputed to repel aphids and moles. To Zone 3 or 4, depending on variety.

Anemone *(Anemone)*

Anemones can give you colour (a wide range, from delicate pinks, blues, and whites to vibrant mauves and reds) from early spring until the summer. They're quite unpromising-looking tubers — they've been compared to stones and to dried leather — but they produce fabulous flowers. Soak the tubers overnight in warm water before planting. In very cold regions, you'll need to lift some of the more tender varieties in the fall. Zones vary, depending on type.

Crocus *(Crocus)*

For many people, the blooming of the crocus is the true sign of spring. Many varieties won't survive in very cold areas. Gardeners who live in these regions could try *C. vernus* 'Purpureus Grandiflorus' or other selections of *C. vernus* in order to enjoy these cheerful little flowers in shades of yellow, white, purple, and blue. They grow to a height of about 10 cm (4 inches). Planted in a sunny, sheltered spot, crocuses will bloom as soon as the snow disappears. Unfortunately, they're a favourite of squirrels, which find all their parts — flowers, leaves, and bulbs — equally tasty. Try planting your corms a bit deeper than usual — this sometimes help to protect them from squirrels and chipmunks. Zones vary, depending on variety.

Fritillaria *(Fritillaria)*

If squirrels are the bane of your gardening existence, try the *Fritillaria imperialis*. Squirrels and other creatures that enjoy gnawing on bulbs don't like the taste, so plant it near other bulbs they usually devour. It grows to 90 cm (3 feet), with bright orange, red, or yellow blooms, and prefer a spot that's sunny and well drained. Flowers in early spring. Hardy to Zone 5.

Another fritillaria is snake's head (*F. meleagris*). It looks at home in an informal setting and lends itself to naturalizing. Plant it in sun or light shade. It blooms in early spring through to May, and holds its purple, bell-shaped blossoms on an arching stem. It will reach about 30 cm (1 foot) in height. To Zone 5.

Glory of the Snow *(Chionodoxa luciliae)*

Glory of the snow has small starry flowers that will open even when there is snow on the ground. Its flowers are violet to blue, with a deep-blue midrib. Once they have finished blooming, they leave behind foliage that looks like grass. If you leave the foliage uncut, the plant will seed itself, and in a few years you'll have a pretty mass of colour in the spring. Plant in a sunny spot with well-drained soil. Grows to about 10 to 15 cm (4 to 6 inches). To Zone 2.

Fritillaria (TOP LEFT); *daffodil* (TOP RIGHT); *glory of the snow* (MIDDLE LEFT); *netted iris* (MIDDLE RIGHT); *crocus* (BOTTOM LEFT); *allium* (BOTTOM RIGHT)

Glory of the snow

Hyacinths *(Hyacinthus)*

The sweet-scented flowers of hyacinth come in blue, pink, white, or pale yellow, and are borne on rather stiff stems. The plants grow to 20 or 30 cm (8 to 12 inches). Place in a well-drained, sunny spot. Mulch in Zone 5.

Grape Hyacinth *(Muscari armeniacum)*

If you live in an area where hyacinths don't survive well, such as on the prairies, try grape hyacinths. They come in purple and white varieties, grow to about 30 cm (1 foot), and flower in early spring to midspring. They multiply quickly and their dying foliage is quite unobtrusive. Plant them in a sunny or partly shaded spot. If you see them putting out leaves in the fall, don't bother about them—they're not trying to rush the season. To Zone 4.

Narcissus *(Narcissus)*

Another harbinger of spring, the narcissus family includes daffodils and jonquils. You could say that the range of colour is limited—mainly yellow, with some whites—but the variations on this theme are truly amazing, everything from reddish golds to pale, creamy yellows to pure whites. The sizes vary considerably—from 7 cm (3 inches) to 36 cm (14 inches). Grow in full sun or light shade. Every seven or eight years, dig up the bulbs and divide to prevent overcrowding. Zone 4.

Netted Iris *(Iris reticulata)*

Another early bloomer—late winter or early spring, depending on where you live. It bears attractive purple flowers with yellow markings on stems that grow to 25 or 40 cm (10 to 15 inches). They are hardy, and will multiply over the years. Zone 5.

Plant bulbs to a depth that's 2½ to 3 times their height.

Plants bulbs in groups for the best effect, mixing different kinds for continuous spring colour.

Cover with garden soil, adding some blood meal to deter squirrels.

As with any newly planted material, water well.

Scilla (*Scilla siberica*)

This easy-to-grow bulb is happy in full sun or partial shade, and grows to 15 cm (6 inches). It produces bright-blue hanging bells in early spring in milder zones, but doesn't appear until May in the prairies. It will spread over the years to form a lovely blue springtime carpet. Zone 4.

Snowdrops (*Galanthus*)

This is among the earliest bulbs to bloom, often valiantly pushing its way above the snow. Its small, downward-facing white flowers nod on stems that can grow from 15 to 23 cm (6 to 9 inches), depending on the variety. Zone 4.

Tulips (*Tulipa*)

Choose tulips from early-flowering, midseason-flowering, and late-flowering species to get a long blooming period. Tulips are available in nearly any colour your heart desires, and heights vary, as well. *Tulipa tarda* is a low-growing species of tulip, with bright yellow-and-white petals that open in the sun and stay closed on cloudy days. Zones vary, depending on variety.

Winter Aconite (*Eranthus hyemalis*)

The small, rounded yellow blooms in early spring are surrounded by frills of foliage, and make a nice pairing with snowdrops. They grow to 5 or 10 cm (2 to 4 inches) and prefer light shade. Good for the rock garden, naturalized in the lawn, or in drifts in flower beds. Zone 4.

Rejuvenating and Propagating Bulbs

Over the years, bulbs will begin to produce fewer and smaller flowers. This is usually a sign that the bulb needs to be lifted so that you can replant any new offshoots. How frequently you undertake this lifting will depend on the bulb, not on the calendar. If your bulbs are producing fewer blooms and more foliage, dig them up and divide them in late summer or early fall. Take off the small bulblets that have formed around the main bulb and replant the bulblets. If they are very small, they may take a couple of years to flower, but many will produce the following year.

Revisiting the Cold Frame

- Watering needs will decrease in the early fall for crops planted in midsummer. As their growth slows in the autumn, start to hold back on the water.
- If you are preparing to transplant seedlings into the frame and it's otherwise empty, keep the lid closed for several days to get the soil warm. Plant the seedlings that will grow the tallest at the back of the frame.
- If you have room in the cold frame in among the turnips, carrots, and spinach (you might have already started harvesting some of these!), sow seeds for salad crops, such as lettuce, arugula, cress, and corn salad. (See Chapter 7 for a description of these and other such crops you can start in the cold frame at this time of year.)

Hyacinth

Kids' Gardening: Seeds

Let's look at what kids can do with seeds in the dog days of summer.

Planting Seeds

Your child may already have been introduced to the wonder of seeds if he or she has had a garden plot this summer. Just because the season is winding down doesn't mean that the fun of growing things should stop.

With your child, collect seeds from annuals such as cosmos or coreopsis. Plant them in pots and leave them outside until the weather threatens to become frosty. Move them indoors for wintering over in a sunny window. Some plants may not survive all winter, but let your child experiment with those that are successful and those that aren't. What makes the difference? What are the different requirements of the plants? In the spring, plant out those that are healthy.

Seeds for the Birds

After your child eats a juicy watermelon, encourage him or her to save the seeds. Wash them, dry them, and keep them in an airtight container until the winter. When you get out your bird feeder, you'll have some free seeds for the birds. The seeds from vegetables such as pumpkins, squashes, and cantaloupes can also be used to attract cardinals, chickadees, bluejays, and nuthatches.

Seed Art

Make a mosaic picture with seeds. With your child, gather as many seeds as possible from the garden. Raid the kitchen, as well, for dried peas, peppercorns, rice, dried beans, sunflower seeds, whole cloves, coffee beans, whole coriander, and seeds from melons, pumpkin, squash, oranges, grapefruit, and lemons. Wash and dry the seeds from the fruits and vegetables.

The background material for your picture can be heavy cardboard, plywood, cork, thin wood, or something similar. Any wood used should be sanded smooth to avoid splinters and slivers. Draw a simple design on the background material. As you do so, consider which seeds will work best in each area. Choose seeds of the appropriate colour, size, and shape for each section.

Now you're ready to start applying the seeds. Work on one section at a time. Paint each section with glue as you go. Position the seeds with tweezers, covering the surface of each section well. When you've finished, fill in any bits that are too bare. Spraying the finished picture with a clear varnish will give the piece a glossy appearance.

September Gardening Checklist

Ornamental Garden

- Divide perennials. Plant and transplant perennials such as peonies and lilies this month and next.
- Lift gladiolus corms when leaves have turned brown.
- Buy spring bulbs and store in cool place until planting out next month.
- Continue taking cuttings of plants such as geraniums, impatiens, begonias, and fuchsia. The first three will make good winter houseplants on a sunny windowsill.
- Take hardwood cuttings for propagating.
- Gather seeds from crops you want to propagate.
- Prepare and seed new lawns.
- Rake lawns, remove thatch, and aerate if needed.
- Lift and divide perennials.
- Plant evergreens.
- Keep evergreens and transplanted shrubs and perennials well watered.
- Clean up plant debris. If it's diseased, don't add to compost pile.
- Move tender herbs and houseplants indoors after you've isolated the plants and sprayed them with an insecticidal soap, including underside of leaves and stems. Leave in isolation for two weeks before introducing into the house.

Zones 2 to 6

- After the first light frost, lift and store summer bulbs.

Zones 7 to 9

- Continue deadheading.
- Plant sweet peas, poppies, and cornflowers for early summer flowering next year.
- Prepare new beds for roses to be planted in November and for planting trees and shrubs in the winter.
- Prune heathers that have finished flowering.

Fruit and Vegetable Garden

- Take unripened tomatoes indoors for ripening.
- Sow more winter vegetables, lettuce, spinach, Swiss chard, and kale.

Zones 2 to 6

- Take cuttings of bush fruits.
- As vegetable bed is cleared, sow winter cover crops if late-season crops are not to be grown.

Zones 7 to 9

- Mulch heat-loving crops and protect with season-extending devices to prolong production.

Autumn

"Today is the first day of the rest of your life."

I don't know who said it first, but I wouldn't blame this person a bit for refusing to come forward to claim credit. Like so many sayings that come and go, this one has lost some of its original impact.

What this has to do with the last season in your garden calendar will become clear in a moment. For now, let's just take a look at autumn in Canadian gardens, and why you can become an "autumn gardening convert."

This section was the most exciting of all to write, for the simple reason that it has the greatest potential in terms of season extending. Days get shorter; leaves turn colour and fall off their hosts' limbs; annual plants die with the frost, or just finish and go to seed. An unattended yard can look a mess in short order, and last year's compost beckons, as does a visit to your chiropractor shortly thereafter!

The attraction to fall gardening lies in the fact that your garden is changing — not dying. Days are shorter, but the sun still shines (usually), and the lawn requires less frequent mowings, which suits me just fine, as the thrill of the first cut of spring has long since worn off. I am eager to get my hands dirty again. The cool fall air is much more suitable to garden "work," and the challenge of extending the pleasures and rewards deeper into the season (which is what the book is all about) makes me want to get on with things:

Garden-fresh potatoes and steamed carrots at Christmas.

Red ripe tomatoes till mid-December.

Colourful geraniums that bloom through the winter.

"Fall is the *first* season in the gardening calendar."

I'll lay claim to this saying — but, please — just between you and me and these precious pages.

Chapter 10

October

The Harvest Month

Now is the time to do what people call "putting the garden to bed." Somehow that has a note of finality to it that isn't in keeping with those of us who are interested in extending the gardening season. We're going to keep on going—it's just in a different direction at this time of year. We'll be finishing the harvesting, the cold frame will be in active use, and more of our gardening will be moving indoors. Nevertheless, there *are* some housekeeping duties that should be performed in the garden to ensure that next year's flowers, fruits, and vegetables are as beautiful and delicious as can be.

Fall Care of Perennials

While you've been working in the garden over the summer, you've been cutting back perennials as they finish their blooming, and often getting a second set of blooms as a reward. But now most perennials have truly finished for the season. Get out the clippers or secateurs and start cleaning up the dying stems and leaves.

Prune plants with thick stems to about 25 cm (10 inches). This height will help to catch the snow, which as you know acts as a mulch. Don't be too quick with the cutting, though. You might want to leave some taller stalks as perches for the birds that will visit your garden in the winter, or just for the look of the dried foliage and seed heads against the snow. Plants with softer stems and leaves can be cut down almost to the ground. Any plant that still has green leaves may well be evergreen, so leave it for the winter to provide a bit more colour.

If rainfall has been light in the previous two or three weeks, give the perennials a deep watering.

If you live where a January thaw or chinook weather is likely, make sure you protect your plants with a good mulch such as straw or wood chips when the ground has frozen—perhaps not until next month.

Garden Clean-up

The following tasks can be spread over this month and the next. Let the conditions in your area be your guide.

- In the vegetable garden, remove all plant material that has finished producing, as well as all weeds.
- In late October or early November, give a final application of superslow-release 10-4-4 fertilizer to your grass.

Chrysanthemums hold on even after a few frosts. The mounds of colour brighten the garden as I go about my chores.

- Clean equipment such as fertilizer spreaders and sprayers by flushing all parts well with water and letting them dry before reassembling. Lubricate all moving parts.
- To prevent rusting on hand tools, rub all metal parts with oil.
- Gather all plant stakes, cleaning off any soil that adheres, tie them and store.
- Use plastic coiled tree guards, narrow-meshed chicken wire, or tar-impregnated tree wrap to protect trunks against damage from rabbits and mice. Extend the guard well above the usual snow level in your area.
- If you have a hedge growing along a street that receives a lot of salt in the winter, make a double-layer burlap screen to protect the plants.
- After the first few frosts, mound soil up around rose bushes to a height of about 20 to 30 cm (8 to 12 inches). Remove the soil gradually in the spring when new growth appears.
- Mulch young evergreens, shrubs, and trees.

Another Look at Mulching

Because of our weather conditions in most of Canada, we have to use mulches strategically. I've explained how, in the spring, it's often better to hold back on mulching until the ground has warmed up.

As we move into winter, mulches are used for holding warmer air close to dormant crops to prevent them from freezing solidly, and for keeping the ground loose and protected from the freeze-thaw-freeze cycle.

Don't mulch anything other than tender seedlings from a second sowing of late vegetables or late-summer sowings until after the first hard frost. Use mulch with row covers or individual cloches to keep the frost from nipping leaves.

Once the first hard frost has hit — some gardeners wait until the ground has frozen to about 1.25 cm ($^1/_2$ inch) — start mulching again. Use materials with a loose texture, such as hay or straw, and apply about 30 to 60 cm (1 to 2 feet) of them. Other mulching materials that you can use at this time of year include coarse, well-rotted sawdust, wood chips, and leaves.

Preparing Your Beds for Next Year

We've come almost full circle. We're back at that important subject — improving the soil. This is the best time of year for undertaking this job, whether your garden is new, several years old and well nourished, or being renovated.

The recipe for success is simple. Dig over the area, turning any clumps of sod top down. Don't break them up or shake weeds and grass free. If you want, add a layer of mulch. Until now, I've spoken of the freeze-thaw-freeze cycle in a negative way, but for once I'm going to give it some credit: over the winter, the forces of nature will work on the new bed, freezing and thawing and breaking the clods down. In the spring, turn the soil again, taking out any grass clumps, and work in compost.

When the ground has frozen, mulch perennial beds and shrubs. In areas of the country where the ground usually doesn't freeze, mulch anytime this month.

If weeds continue to be a problem in the fall, don't give up in despair. Keep pulling them and mulch any beds that will lie fallow for the winter.

Sowing Cover Crops

Cover crops are grown for the sole purpose of enriching the soil. They are planted on land that is lying unused, often because its crops have been harvested for the season. They are usually quick growing, and are turned under before they go to seed. You don't have to be a farmer with hundreds of hectares in order to use cover crops (also called green manure) as a device for enriching your soil, keeping weeds down by shading them out, reducing reliance on chemical fertilizers, and best of all lessening the amount of work you have to do in the spring.

Cover crops can raise the organic content of a bed by almost 4 percent and protect the surface of the soil from erosion. The roots help the soil absorb more moisture, and crops that have deep roots aerate and enrich the subsoil, bringing up minerals for use by the new crops. Legume crops have the additional benefit of fixing nitrogen in the soil.

In most regions of Canada, winter cover crops should be sown no later than the middle of October so that the plants can become established before winter sets in. Barley, oats, winter rye, annual rye-grass, clover, and wheat are crops that are suitable for fall planting. Sow the seed on the bare soil, rake it in, and firm it into the soil with the rake. The seeds will grow quickly, outpacing the weeds. In January the cold weather will kill the crop and the growth will collapse, covering and protecting the topsoil. In the spring, dig or plough in the crop, or pull or rake off the dead growth of annual crops, and you're ready to plant the garden. It's not necessary to dig up the dead roots — they add organic matter and help to aerate the soil.

For hardy cover crops — those that don't die in the winter — dig in the crops or pull up the plants in spring, shake the soil off the roots, throw the plants on the compost, rake the bed, and plant. Obviously, this is practical only if you're gardening on a small bed. Larger areas have to be tilled mechanically.

After you dig in or till the fall cover crop in the spring, let the bed sit for two or three weeks before you plant it, to allow the crop time to start decomposing.

ABOVE LEFT:
Protect young trees from nibblers such as mice and rabbits by applying guards to trunks.

ABOVE RIGHT:
The life cycle of the garden continues. Waste from the garden, plentiful at this time of year, will become food for plants as weather and time do their work in breaking it down.

Forcing Plants for Winter Colour

As we head into winter, you don't have to rely on houseplants alone to give you colour and that wonderful feeling of nurturing a growing plant. Forcing bulbs is a traditional method for bringing the sights and scents of spring into your home in the winter. And don't confine this just to *your* home — Christmas is coming, so make up some pretty pots of bulbs to give to friends.

If you haven't tried forcing bulbs before, the easiest to force are narcissus, hyacinth, *Iris reticulata*, grape hyacinth, and tulips marked as being good for forcing. A bit more difficult are snowdrops, scilla, and glory of the snow.

Preparing the bulbs: Many plants need a dormant period in a cool, dark place (for outdoor bulbs, that's underground) in order to be ready to produce lavish blossoms in the growing season. Bulbs for forcing are no different, so you'll need to hide your forcing bulbs away for a while to recreate those conditions.

As soon as possible after you've bought the bulbs, pot them up in an all-purpose potting mix. (Most forcing bulbs are planted in soil, but paperwhites are usually forced in water. I'll outline the steps for planting in soil here; see the entry for paperwhites to find out about forcing in water.) If you can't do this right away, take them out of their packaging and store them in a *dark*, cool, dry place until you can plant them.

Any well-drained container will do for planting as long as it's twice as deep as the bulbs you are planting. Fill the pot loosely with soil, then add the bulbs so the tips are at rim level; the final soil level will be just below the rim and the noses of the bulbs will be visible. Plant most bulbs closely together — as many as six or seven in a 15 cm (6-inch) diameter pot; daffodils and paperwhites are happiest with about 2.5 to 5 cm (1 to 2 inches) of space between them. Gently firm down the soil and water well. Label the pots.

The bulbs now go into a dark place with a constant temperature between 3 and 10°C (35 and 50°F). If you have a basement refrigerator, they can be stored there. Some people keep them in the garage, though you should cover the pots with wire mesh if mice or squirrels can get at them. A cool basement room will also work. If there's any danger of light reaching the bulbs, cover the containers with newspaper, an inverted cardboard box, or some other similar device. Check pots to be sure that the soil is still moist.

The length of time that you leave bulbs in this cool spot will depend on the variety you're forcing and how long it takes the root system to form (see the plant list that follows). You'll know the bulbs are ready to be put in the light when the roots start to emerge from the drainage hole in the pot. There will also be about 2.5 cm (1 inch) of foliage on the smaller bulbs and about 8 cm (3 inches) of foliage on larger bulbs at this stage.

When flower buds start to appear — which could take as long as four weeks, again depending on the variety — move the pots to a sunny location at room temperature.

Bulbs for forcing are planted so their tips are just at the rim. Make sure there's room for the roots by choosing a pot that's at least twice the depth of the bulb.

Cover bulbs with soil, leaving the noses visible for larger bulbs (smaller bulbs would be covered entirely). Label the pots and store in a dark, cool, dry place.

October Gardening Checklist

Ornamental Garden

- Plant spring bulbs and more perennials.
- Continue cutting lawn as long as it grows. Give it a final fertilizing.
- Rake leaves and add to compost, or put in bags to pile around cold frame or compost bin.
- Plant and transplant shrubs, bushes, and trees.
- Dig new beds; add well-rotted compost or manure.
- Protect evergreens and roses in areas with early freeze-up and snowfall (see Chapter 11).
- Prepare bulbs for forcing.
- Winterize lawn mower and sharpen and clean all garden tools.
- Pull up all annuals and put in compost bin.
- Clean borders, then weed and mulch.
- Give a light pruning to rose bushes, including ramblers.
- Make windbreaks for rhododendrons, azaleas, and young shrubs.

Zones 7 to 9

- Lift and store tender bulbs.

Fruit and Vegetable Garden

- Clean off vegetable garden if last crops harvested, making sure to remove plastic mulch; sow cover crop.
- Pot up herbs such as mint, chives, and parsley for indoors.
- Apply Tanglefoot to trees to catch winter moths.
- Give asparagus bed a heavy watering for an early crop in the spring.
- Cut back dead asparagus foliage and add it to the compost. Top-dress both asparagus and rhubarb with 5 cm (2 inches) of well-rotted manure.
- Plant garlic and onions that overwinter.

Zones 2 to 6

- In areas where snow comes early and provides a consistent cover, plant lettuce, parsnips, spinach, Swiss chard, and onions in the last week of this month. Plant twice as deeply and thickly as for a spring planting. You could have crops two to four weeks earlier than with a spring planting.

Zones 7 to 9

- Sow a final crop of lettuce in ground or in cold frame.
- Take cuttings of bush fruits.
- Prune canes that have fruited.
- Divide chives.
- Add rotted manure or compost to next year's vegetable bed. Sow cover crops.

Chapter 11

November

A Green Thumb Indoors

You don't need a greenhouse to continue gardening indoors throughout the winter. I won't try to fool you, though — it's not as easy as growing things outdoors. All indoor plants, whether ornamental or edible, are growing in an artificial environment. This puts them under stress, making them more susceptible to the ravages of insects and diseases. So they require special care. Is the extra effort worth it? Absolutely!

One secret to successful indoor gardening is choosing plants that adapt well to the indoor atmosphere. In most Canadian homes, growing a crop of tomatoes indoors is just about impossible, but there are some plants that are worth trying.

The following are some old favourites, plus some more unusual plants for indoor growing. Not all of them need artificial light, but some will do much better with it.

African Violet (Saintpaulia)

This popular houseplant has charming flowers in pink, white, blue, and lavender. It does best in bright, indirect light in summer and direct sun or bright, indirect light in winter. It loves fluorescent lights and hates to be overwatered. Let the soil dry so that the pot feels light when lifted, then give it a good soaking, watering from the bottom with room-temperature water. African violets are one of those plants that like high humidity, but they should not be misted. To provide humidity, put the pot in a bowl of pebbles and add water to about half the depth of the pebbles. The bottom of the pot should not touch the water. They like a temperature of about 16°C (60°F), but will tolerate lows of 13°C (55°F) and highs of 27°C (80°F). Remove dead leaves and flowers. Repot about every two years if the plant is looking overcrowded.

Aloe (Aloe)

A useful plant to grow in the kitchen — use its juice to ease the pain of burns. The succulent leaves of the aloe develop in a rosette fashion, and the plant can quickly outgrow its spot. Give the aloe dry, hot conditions (a bit cooler in the winter) and direct to bright light. Don't water it more often than once a week.

Asparagus Fern (Asparagus setaceus)

Asparagus ferns look great in hanging containers and are very easy to care for. Given filtered light and barely moist soil, they will throw out many long feathery branches. The asparagus fern will tolerate a wide range of temperatures. Keep the plant tidy by cutting back any branches that look ragged.

PHOTOGRAPHS

David Michael Allen:

14–15, 18 left, 21 right, 33 bottom right, 36, 45–50, 51 right, 52–56, 60–63, 73, 74, 80–85, 89, 90, 96, 102, 103, 130, 134–137, 138 left, 144, 145 right, 151 right, 153, 161, 176, 185 bottom, 187, 190 right, 194, 195, 198–204, 207 top right, 208 bottom, 209, 210, 217 left, 218, 219, 221 top, 221 bottom left, 223, 224, 228, 231, 236 right, 239 top, 241–244

Greg Holman:

Introduction, How to Use This Book, 10–13, 16, 18 right, 27–31, 33 bottom left, 34, 39, 43, 51 left, 59 top, 67, 76, 79, 87, 88, 97, 101 top, 121, 145 left, 152, 156, 159 top, 169, 171 top left and bottom, 179, 181 bottom, 182, 193, 205, 213, 215, 217 right, 227 right, 233, 234, 239 bottom

Joe Lepiano:

Title Page 17, 20 bottom left, 23 left, 59 bottom, 65, 69, 71, 77, 95, 101 bottom, 105, 108, 110 right, 112, 113, 116, 119 left, 122–126, 133, 138 right, 140, 149 tent caterpillar, 157, 159 bottom, 166, 173, 181 top, 185 top, 186, 227 top left and bottom, 230, 236 left

Weall & Cullen Nurseries:

20 top left and left centre, 21 left, 22 left centre, 23 right, 24, 25 top, 72, 86, 91–93, 119 right (All-America Selections), 142, 163, 164 bottom, 168, 171 top right and right centre, 183, 184, 189, 196, 197, 229

Other:

19 Daryl Benson/Masterfile; 20 top right Robert Ritchie/Niagara Parks Commission Botanical Gardens and School of Horticulture; 22 top left and bottom, top right, 25 bottom Glen P. Lumis, Professor, Dept. of Horticultural Science, University of Guelph; 40 Freeman Patterson/Masterfile; 94 Robert Ritchie/Niagara Parks Commission Botanical Gardens and School of Horticulture; 98 Gay Bumgarner/Tony Stone Images; 107, 109 Dr. Mary Ruth McDonald, Ontario Ministry of Agriculture, Food and Rural Affairs, Muck Research Station; 110 left AAFC, London Research Centre; 111, 114 Dr. Mary Ruth McDonald, Ontario Ministry of Agriculture, Food and Rural Affairs, Muck Research Station; 115 Agincourt Garden Club; 117 Dr. Mary Ruth McDonald, Ontario Ministry of Agriculture, Food and Rural Affairs, Muck Research Station; 146 top Canadian National Collection of Insects/Centre for Land and Biological Resources Research; 146 centre Ontario Ministry of Agriculture, Food, and Rural Affairs; 146 bottom Agriculture Canada; 147 (cabbageworm, cankerworm, cutworm, flea beetle, leaf miner) Canadian National Collection of Insects/Centre for Land and Biological Resources Research; 147 (flea-beetle damage, larval cabbage-maggot damage, adult cucumber beetle, grasshopper) AAFC, London Research Centre; 147 (green peach aphid, adult codling moth) Agriculture Canada; 147 (leaf-hopper damage) Ontario Ministry of Agriculture, Food, and Rural Affairs; 149 (leaf-roller) Canadian National Collection of Insects/Centre for Land and Biological Resources Research; 149 (whitefly damage, sawfly pupa) Ontario Ministry of Agriculture, Food, and Rural Affairs; 149 (mealybug, juniper scale, thrips damage) Agriculture Canada; 149 (slug, Colorado potato beetle, wireworm, hornworm, white grub) AAFC, London Research Centre; 151 left AAFC, London Research Centre; 154 top Neal & Mary Mishler/Tony Stone Images; 164 top Robert Ritchie/Niagara Parks Commission Botanical Gardens and School of Horticulture; 167 Dr. Mary Ruth McDonald, Ontario Ministry of Agriculture, Food and Rural Affairs, Muck Research Station; 170 Glen P. Lumis, Professor, Dept. of Horticultural Science, University of Guelph; 174 bottom Agriculture Canada; 174 top AAFC, London Research Centre; 175 Agriculture Canada; 206, 207 all (except top right); 208 left Photo Courtesy Internationaal Bloembollen Centram, Hillegom, Holland; 212 Curtis Lantigna; 221 bottom right Photo Courtesy Internationaal Bloembollen Centram, Hillegom, Holland

ILLUSTRATIONS

Margo Stahl:
33 top, 128, 129, 154 bottom, 190 left

Special thanks to:

David and Arlene Carter
Charlotte and Lawrence Cullen
Sandi and Robert Chapple
Erica Cohen
Russ Gomme
Ann Holman
Rosemary Kilbourn
Jearld Moldenhauer
Mary Mordy
Karen and David Spagnolo
Mrs. Stanoulis
Andy Vaidilla
Rae Zimmer

Contributing Editor: Wendy Thomas

Editorial Co-ordinator: Lorraine Johnson

Assignment Photography: David Michael Allen
Greg Holman

Art Direction and Design: Joe Lepiano/Pronk&Associates

Copy Editor: Beverly Sotolov

Proofreader: Alison Reid

Horticultural Editor: Dennis Flanagan

Jacket Design: Pronk&Associates

Produced by Pronk&Associates